The In Sync™ Dog Training Method

6 Secrets to Unleashing Your Dog's Greatest Potential and Your Own

By Alecia Evans, PDT, MA, Inventor

DEDICATION

To Spirit: thank you for this amazing playground of wonder you have created for us all to experience the miraculous connections with all our relations.

ACKNOWLEDGMENTS

I thank Pepe and Brandy, Tuscon and Barney, Indie and Aiyana, Cleo and Julie and Wolfie: you all blessed my life in the most extraordinary ways and taught me the gift of being a humane human. Thank you for giving me back my inner sight, my telepathic abilities, and reconnecting me with the true heart of all my relations. Here and in spirit you always live in my heart and I carry on your teachings each day.

I would like to acknowledge all of my four-legged and two-legged clients over the years and thank you for allowing me into your lives, for trusting me with your precious selves, and for allowing me to become aware of the essence we share.

To my precious niece and nephew, Jordy and Matty, I acknowledge the magic contained within you both. May the wisdom, connection and oneness with the animal kingdom stay strong in your hearts and the hearts of all mankind.

I give thanks and gratitude for Norman Gershman who inspired me and nudged me to walk the journey of Walk In Sync. Thanks for giving me the space to grow up.

I am so grateful to all of my spiritual teachers and guides 2 legged and 4 for awakening me to the truth of who I am.

With deep love and adoration, I thank Andrea Bejarano and Dr. Nan Lu for opening my heart and teaching me to cultivate the deep essence contained within by bringing me home to the Tao. It was your teachings that reconnected me with my love of the natural world and back to my the gift I have with the animals.

And most of all, I would like to thank my mother and sister for always loving me, even when they didn't know what in the world I was talking about.

CONTENTS

The In Sync™ Dog Training Method is unique in its approach as the information you will receive comes directly from the dogs. I simply translated it on their behalf. Most training systems will teach you what you need to teach your dog, making it about your dog. I will share with you information based on the energy you need to embody for your dog to see you and accept you as an authentic leader, making it about you. Think of it as dog training from an inside out approach.

Since the Walk In Sync™ Tools were developed along with the In Sync™ Method, I feel it important to share with you how the tools evolved as they provided me with the foundation for teaching the In Sync™ Method. In addition, it provides me with an opportunity to share with you the path along which they evolved as I sense many of you will be able to see a bit of yourself along the way and feel relieved to know that there is a simple solution.

I for one was never a big believer in tools until this system came along and I got to see first- hand how well they worked not only for the dogs but for the humans. My goal from the beginning has been to improve the communication and connection between human and dog in the safest and most humane way possible.

The In Sync™ Training Method is a truly unique in that it is going to be working with you before it works with your dog to assist you in understanding from your dog's mindset what he/she is looking for from you. So often training is based on making the dog do what we say or teaching them commands that please us, so it is more of a one-way conversation. What I am sharing here is the beginning of a two way conversation in training or shaping behaviors where we humans are open to how our dog (god spelled backwards) is helping to shape us into better more Authentic Leaders and more humane humans.

While you may not agree with all contained in the book, I ask you to keep an open mind and simply apply the 6 Secrets with your dog and allow yourself to carry those messages with you throughout the day and notice the changes take place as you do.

My Personal Story: Barney and Me

Have you seen the movie *Marley and Me*? Well, years before it came out, I had Barney, an adorable but out of his mind chocolate lab who very well could have been a grandparent of Marley. The day I went to pick him out he came over to me and my husband at the time, out of all the other pups, began suckling on my finger and laid a big ol fart on me and somehow I was in love. As a pup, he was just the cutest thing on the planet, a soft furry milk chocolate kiss, full of himself and inquisitive without ever feeling the need to listen to anyone but himself.

Barney was so full of energy and playfulness it really made me laugh, like the times he would put the top half of his body in the toilet bowl and try to splash all the water out while it was flushing, or the times he would dig all the water out of his water bowl and try to take a bath in the kitchen by himself, or the time he got into the freeze dried liver treats eating ¾ of the bucket leaving the last ¼ only because he felt so sick. I honestly believe that for the first 3 years of his life he thought his name was, "Barney No"

At about 14 weeks I knew he would have to be trained and I was pretty enthusiastic about getting it all right. So I enrolled him in puppy school, we were told to use a choke collar and training lead and off we went to educate ourselves. We barely passed but he did receive a puppy obedience class certificate and away we went into the journey of our life.

Barney grew quick and with each passing week he got stronger and stronger, and more and more rebellious. I however was not growing stronger and his 75 pounds of torque was a lot more than my 115 pounds of body could handle. Let's just say I never really walked Barney, he was always dragging me somewhere. In the fall of his first year, I became concerned as there was a big hill we needed to walk down to get to the park and I began having visions of being pulled off my feet and sliding or being dragged on the ice down the hill to the park. So I asked around and the trainers that I spoke with suggested a prong collar. They said if the choke chain was not doing it, which it obviously wasn't as Barney still took me for a walk everywhere we went despite gagging the whole way then the prong collar was next.

So off I went to purchase what looked to me like a medieval contraption that would press metal prongs into my dog's neck when he pulled. Immediately my once fearless and over-exuberant 75 pound puppy became fearful. While I noticed that in him, at the time it was getting to the point that it was either him or me. So a little fear in him, while I was able to walk safely seemed like a reasonable compromise. The prong collar worked for a bit but Barney decided to overcome his fear and began pulling through the prong collar anyway. OH JOY!!! Here we were back to me being pulled and him not caring that a 115 pound weight was being dragged behind him. What next?

About 3 weeks after I began using the prong on Barney, my other dog, Tuscon got into a fight with a German Sheppard who had on a prong collar and my index finger got caught in between the prongs and it just about broke my knuckle, which then soured me on using that as a tool.

Back to asking the trainers what else I could use, a nose halter was recommended. Let's just say that Barney was not too pleased with something being on his nose. He jumped and twisted in ways I didn't even know a dog could maneuver. He scratched and clawed his nose bloody and flipped himself all over the concrete ground like he was being tortured by a thousand fire ants. And here I am, his caring human, standing there in shock on the other end of the leash not knowing what else to do. After about a week he accepted the nose halter but I began to notice that he was not walking correctly and upon touching his neck one day he yelped. A trip to the chiropractor revealed that Barney in his fit of dislike had knocked 3 vertebrae out of alignment. LOVELY, I thought. Here I am trying to get my dog to walk with me and somehow the two of us keep getting hurt.

As a last resort, a shock collar was recommended. Not that I wanted to punish the dog at all. I was simply fearful that since I didn't have any control over him whatsoever, that if he took off, he could get hurt, so preventing his pain by causing him a little pain was my line of thinking if it could potentially save his life.

I made sure to test it on my husband at the time and when he didn't keel over from the shock I figured Barney wouldn't either. So one day we went to the park to test it. I have never seen a dog look like they had just jumped outside of their skin. After the first buzz Barney looked like he had just gone mad, the kind of bewildered look one exhibits when they have just experienced something so horrific that has shocked and scared them half wild at the same time and their life has changed forever as they don't know now what is now normal or if they can ever trust again. Needless to say I just wanted to crawl under a rock.

From the moment he first got buzzed Barney was leery of anything electronic for the rest of his life. The first time I shocked him, my heart just broke and it took me years to forgive myself. Barney wore that shock collar just a few times and each time I hated to use it but had no idea what else to do. So I spent another year being led around by that big brown dog.

Having used each of these tools with little success, and with my still growing 90-pound over-exuberant Lab who could not care less that I was attached to him, I had no idea what else to do. What motivated my dog, what made him pull, and what made him stop? I was clueless. The only thing I knew was what the trainer told me to do and so I did it.

So now we were back to the choke chain with a new determination from me to get this dog trained no matter what. By this time I had asked several of the trainers about using treats as Barney was a total food hound but they all looked at me like I had just said the worst possible thing you could ever say to another human and made me feel as if I used a treat I would be struck down dead where I stood by lightening. So the one thing that may have worked was strictly forbidden and we went back to methods of pitting his will against mine.

Turning Point

I had become increasingly frustrated with Barney having tried my best to train this young wildebeest who was nearly ripping my arm out of the socket on every walk.

One day, while Barney and I were out for a walk, okay, while Barney was walking me and I was trying to stay on my feet, out of sheer frustration bordering on rage and getting increasingly sick of being pulled around, I got so mad that I yanked on his choke chain hard four times in a row. When I saw Barney began to cower, my anger turned shame. I had a moment of clarity and in that awareness I knew in my gut there had to be a better way for us to learn how to communicate. There also had to be a better way for me to learn how to be a better leader and to stop failing my dog. It hurt so damn much to feel like I was so clueless. It was a proverbial "come to Jesus" moment for me and I made Barney a promise that one day I would find a better way to work with dogs that would keep them safe, help them communicate better with their people and vice verse, as well as be more respectful of their bodies.

My next call was to an animal behaviorist, who immediately asked me if I had considered using treats. I could not believe what I was hearing. Looking back I think she was at the forefront of the Positive Dog Training movement. Upon our first meeting she pulled a treat out of her pouch and it was like Barney had Bionic hearing and was the most well behaved dog I had ever witnessed.

From then on B and I had a better level of communication. It was as if somehow magically food was tied into his ability to hear me. Yet we had not fully resolved his pulling issues.

What I had yet to discover was that many of Barney's behavior and pulling issues were a direct result of a disconnection to his body caused by me yanking on his neck from the tools I had been using.

Determined to find a better way I read one of Linda Tellington Jones' books on dogs. Linda is a brilliant woman who invented T-Touch and trains people all around the world in this safe, highly effective method of bodywork that instills light back into our cells and allows our animals bodies to heal rapidly and safely. In her book, Linda suggested that dogs on collars and choke chains often become disconnected from their bodies which may be a reason why they are less sensitive to listening to their cues from the collar. To remedy this and reconnect the dog with its innate sensitivity and listening skills she shared a leash wrapping technique to assist the dog. I went out with Barney one day and tried it. I took the leash and wrapped it around the perimeter of Barney's entire body from chest to tail.

While I don't think I was able to master Linda's technique exactly, I did notice one incredible shift. With the leash around Barney's chest and at front leg height Barney would not walk forward until I did. He was actually looking up at me for the first time ever to ask me what we were doing rather than dragging me around. Although it was not comfortable to be able to walk him with the leash wrapped all the way around him in the way that I interpreted it, this situation provided me with the awareness that a dog that is connected to its whole body is better able to hear you than one whose neck has been repeatedly yanked on.

My jaw dropped the first time I did this as Barney wouldn't move forward until I did. Voila!!!!! Bingo!!!!! Radical!!!! OMG!!!! Bells, trumpets and angelic whistles from the heavens. Golden streams of light beaming on us. I had found a way for us to potentially walk together.

Only problem was "how do you walk a dog down the street with his leash wrapped around his body?" Unfortunately, I did not discover a humane training harness during Barney's lifetime, but I pledged that someday I would find a better way for all dogs to be trained. Although I did not know it at the time, this one "aha" moment would direct me to asking the questions that would lead me to the creation of the Walk In Sync™ Humane Dog Walking and Training System and the In Sync™ Training Method.

Keeping My Promise to Barney

Around the age of 21, fresh out of college I began my 15 year career as an Elite Fitness Trainer in a well-known Upper West Side Health Club. It was there that I met my first spiritual teacher on the fitness floor while correcting her posture for a particular exercise. I had no idea then the journey I would begin or that it would end up almost 20 years later in the writing of this book.

During our initial training sessions she would give me certain exercises to do for my mind that unbeknownst to me were the beginning of my meditation practice and the quieting of my mind that would ultimately lead me to the vision and creation of the Walk In Sync™ Humane Dog Walking and Training System and the In Sync™ Method.

I made the switch from training humans to training dogs about a decade later. During my Fitness Career I had become an expert in human biomechanics (the way the body moves through space in proper posture and alignment). I transferred all of that valuable knowledge to the dogs when I began training them. I took a massage course for animals, studied dog anatomy and physiology from books and began paying very close attention to the animals gait or movement patterns and its effect on their health and behavior.

I began observing that most of the traditional training tools we use are not biomechanically correct for the dogs and were causing some misalignment issues of neck vertebrae and neck tissue that was effecting their natural behaviors.

About 6 years into it I began asking, "What would it take to create a totally humane training system that would never harm or choke another dog or puppy again and make the world a safer and more respectful place for them?" A year later a harness showed up that gave me the awareness that it was possible to no longer choke dogs while training.

I sold a lot of those harnesses to clients but I soon realized the limitation of that harness' design and wanted to create one that would no longer chafe the dogs legs like some of my clients had complained of. Another harness came along that had a similar design except this one limited the stride of the shoulders range of motion which I felt would not be great for a growing puppy, as well as athletic dogs.

A year later while sitting in a meditation I was shown a vision of a new training harness that I had never seen before. Upon further questioning of the "vision giver," I asked, "So what would you like me to do with this?" To which I was given the reply, "create it and teach people to Walk In Harmony with their dogs." "Great", I thought, "This meditation stuff really works." I was so grateful because I love dogs and I was so tired of them having to be choked to teach them.

Little did I know the path I would have to walk to bring Walk In Sync™ to fruition.

After my initial thought of, "Great," the reality dawned on me that it takes money to create a product, of which at the time I had little extra. So I made a pact with the "vision giver," if you send me the people and the money to make this happen, I will follow your lead and bring this to life as largely as you would like it to go to transform the world into a more humane place for dogs. I did not know at the time that it would transform their humans as well.

Just by taking my first step of saying, "YES," and asking the questions, "What else is possible?! and "What would it take for a humane system to show up with total ease, joy and grace?!", and then a series of angels dropped into my life to make this dream a reality.

With each step, I had no idea how the next would unfold, who would show up or what would take place. I honestly can say that Walk In Sync™ has been a true walk of faith that what was needed would show up. Since the time I learned to meditate and then began an intense Qi Gong practice I remembered my teacher telling me that all the answers lie within, so when I did not know I found a place to sit, close my eyes, go within, get clear about what I was asking for, let go and then be quiet and listen and pay attention to what was being shown. And with a heart full of gratitude and faith I kept walking in sync with the "vision giver."

All the pieces of the puzzle started fitting into place. To date, while it has not always been an easy walk as it has tested every ounce of my faith and courage. I continue walking in sync with the "vision giver" and not only is the product flying off the shelves it is making the world a more humane place for dogs.

I am so happy to say that I have kept my promise to Barney with the creation of the Walk In Sync™ Humane Dog Walking and Training System and In Sync™ Method. I know that he has watched over this whole endeavor, especially on those days when I was so tired and frustrated that I felt finished with this creation, it was Barney who kept pulling me along to continue going. Maybe that's what he had been doing all along.

It is my heart's highest intention that the In Sync™ Method will in some way(s) inspire and empower you on your own path of not only learning the 6 Secrets to Unleashing Your Dog's Greatest Potential, but incorporating it into your life to unleash your own greatest potential.

Paws Up! And keep Walking In Sync!

Alecia Evans, HDT, MA, Animal Healer, Inventor

INTRODUCTION

"I've seen a look in dogs' eyes, a quickly vanishing look of amazed contempt, and I am convinced that basically dogs think humans are nuts."
- John Steinbeck

Why Traditional Training Tools Are Not Safe for Your Dog

When I began training my dogs over 22 years ago I was told by various trainers to use a nylon neck collar and then in order to stop them from pulling to purchase and use choke chains, when that did not work to place a metal prong collar around my dog's neck and when that didn't work to use a nylon nose halti on my dogs nose to stop them from pulling, finally I was told to resort to a shock collar when all the other tools failed.

It took me years of direct experience and observation to realize that the time has come to change the tools we are using to walk and train dogs and puppy's to be biomechanically correct, safer and more effective for the canines and their humans.

From Tragedy to Triumph

It was frustrating, scary, embarrassing, and sometimes painful for those two years when I got yanked off my feet because Barney saw another dog or a squirrel. I had no control over that dog at all. I definitely took it personally and got mad at him. I mean how could a dog who received so much love not love me back enough to respect me? Seriously, I was clueless about what dogs knew or how they thought.

Many dog parents have experienced the same frustrations for more than 60 years. During that time, few long-term studies have been conducted reviewing the potential damage those training tools can cause to the dog's neck, throat, spine, esophagus, or eyes. Far fewer veterinarians have taken the time to see if their dog clients are being treated in the most humane manner during training. And even fewer dog trainers—the front line of protection for dogs—have questioned whether the tools we use for training are physically or psychologically harming the four-legged members of our families. The good news is that this is all changing.

Below is an excerpt from a study I discovered years after my experience with Barney, confirming what I had begun behaviorally observing in the dogs and pups I was training which was leading me to believe that not all behavioral issues stem from the dog being a "bad" dog. In most cases (98% of what I have observed in my clients) the dog was a great dog, it was simply out of alignment somewhere in its spine and that misalignment was causing a disruption in the dogs energy that was not allowing the dogs energy to flow properly thus creating a "shorter fuse" to which the dog was reacting thus leading to the behavioral issue, not the reverse.

This information is from a 1992 study of 400 dogs that appeared in The: "Animal Behaviour Consultants Newsletter" July,1992 V.9 No 2. A. Dog Owners were offered a free examination of their dog by a Chiropractor in return for their voluntary participation. Those who volunteered to participate in the Study had mostly ordinary dogs, in that; owners presented them without any suspicion of spinal anomalies... Canine back problems are common.

ALARMING FACTS FROM THE STUDY

63% of the dogs examined had neck and spinal injuries.

78% of the dogs with aggression or over activity problems had neck and spinal injuries.
Of the dogs with neck injuries, 91% had experienced hard jerks on a leash or had strained against their leashes.

The results of the Study show that the Chiropractors found back anomalies in 63% of the 400 dogs. **Dogs that 'acted out', in other words, that exhibited over activity and aggression; 78% had spinal anomalies. Spinal anomalies seem to constitute an irritation that often results in stress reactions, aggression or fear.**

Mr. Hallgren found that this was also in accordance with his own and his Students experience as Behaviorists, with problematic dogs. In the Study there were some factors that correlated with spinal anomalies. These were: - Accidents Pulling on Leash (see below) Limping During Adolescence

Pulling on Leash: Of those dogs that had cervical (neck) anomalies, 91% had been exposed to harsh jerks on the leash, or they had a long history of pulling or straining at the end of a leash. There is a risk of 'whip-lash' from jerking the leash that probably increases if the dog wears a choke chain collar. Choke chain collars are constructed such that; pulling it results in pressure distributed around the dog's neck, but, the muscles that absorb the pressure are situated mostly at the sides of the neck. The neck and throat are almost unprotected.

Additional Comment by Mr. Hallgren...

Choke Chain Collars can be dangerous. For many years others and I have criticized the use of choke chain collars and training methods that use jerking and pulling on a leash as a means of controlling behavior. Unfortunately, most dog trainers use just this technique. There is probably a relationship between the force of the jerk and the risk of injury. I believe dog owners should be warned that chaining a dog to anything firm, that isn't elastic, without surveillance may increase the risk of a spinal injury. A dog can easily forget the boundaries of the chain or rope, accelerate, and suddenly come to a halt, with all the stopping power concentrated around the dog's neck. **The Study concludes that; leash corrections, the dog forging ahead or a tethered dog hitting the end of a solid line may inflict spinal injury.**

While I will not impose my point of view here any further I think you can see from the study that the risk of using neck based tools are pretty high.

Recently I have come across the work of two veterinarians who are taking this issue seriously are Dr. Peter Dobias and Dr. Karen Becker.

Please see appendix A. Page 102

Walk in Your Dog's Paw

When I ask my clients how they would feel if I placed a metal choke chain around their neck and then yanked on it, most look at me like I'm off my rocker. Perhaps it's the visual of the pain of throat constriction, coupled with their eyeballs bulging out of their head as the soft tissue and cartilage of their neck is instantly and painfully constricted.

All of my clients look horrified at the possibility and writhe at the thought of the pain. So I then ask them why they think it is okay to put that very same choke chain around their dogs' necks. Didn't they think that their dogs could feel the identical pain? A disturbed look comes over most of their faces when they realize that this is what they have subjected their dogs to because they did not know what else to choose. They were just doing what they were told by the trainer without questioning it.

Throughout my years of being a dog guardian, I have used every training tool and device on the market. The one I felt worst about was the shock collar. The one I feel most embarrassed about was the choke chain. In more than a decade of dog training, I have never had to use either again. While I have successfully trained thousands of dogs of all breeds, ages, sizes, personalities, and temperaments, I have always sought a better way to train that would fully respect the dog and his or her body while never doing him/her any harm.

It is important to note that even a plain ol' flat collar can be a danger to your dog if they are allowed to continue pulling on it and choking themselves with it. If looked at from a purely physiological standpoint, anything around your dog or puppy's neck that could potentially choke them is not too safe. While I do advocate that every dog needs a collar on their neck to carry their tags, a harness seems far safer for training and walking.

We can wait for years to see if further research validates what appears to be a pretty common sense answer to choke or not to choke in the name of training or we can just change it now. Science seems to spend A LOT of money attempting to validate common sense. My philosophy has always been KISS: Keep It Simple Silly. If common sense makes a difference then use it, it's way less expensive, takes a much shorter time and gets results a lot quicker. Science can catch up later, but I for one am not willing to take the chance with my dog or puppy's body or that of any of my clients till they do.

How the Practice of an Ancient Chinese Self-Healing Art Brings about a Change of Heart

During my years of Qigong (the ancient self-healing martial art) practice, I became highly attuned to the sensitivity of animals. Before that time, although I loved my dog, I thought of him as just a dog—not a creature capable of intelligent thought let alone of feeling pain. As my Qi practice progressed, I began to see and feel animals in a far different way, coming to witness and understand their innate intelligence, their ability to feel pain, and their capacity to experience emotions. What I was now aware of went far beyond anything I had been taught by adults, trainers, and Veterinarians and could possibly imagine. Once I began to realize dogs' capacity for pain and pleasure, excitement and fear, I knew that I had to find the best ways to train without causing any pain or fear in a language that the dog is more comfortable with.

Unfortunately I never did get to use a harness with Barney. When he was about 7 something changed in him and he finally calmed down to the point that I could walk him on and off leash like a gentleman.

About 14 years after my awareness of using safer tools, I came across a front clip harness that actually worked to stop my client's dog Sophie (ironically another Chocolate Lab) from pulling. Unfortunately, it ended up chafing her front legs; and I received the same complaint from my clients. There was one other harness I tried but it, too, had an issue due to the adjustments at the dog's chest line.

If this harness was not adjusted properly, it would sag and then inhibit the dog's or puppy's shoulder stride, limiting the full range of motion. So I began asking the universe for a harness that would work and neither chafe my dog nor would limit the range of motion in his shoulder stride. Little did I know that I would be the one inventing this miracle harness.

Walk In Sync™ is Born

One morning back in October of 2009 while meditating the vision came to me for a harness that would never choke another dog again during the training process and would actually work to alleviate the pulling habit in just minutes by creating solid boundaries that would teach the dog to back off of pressure rather than trying to pull through it.

I have to say that the vision I was shown was really exciting. It appeared that I would be able to educate dogs from puppyhood or adult dogs with habitual behaviors on a system that would never choke them or cause them pain, while allowing them the freedom to learn to harness their energy to unleash their greatest potential. Something deep inside me knew that this harness was going to change the world of dog training and maybe the world forever.

Be careful what you ask for because you just might have to invent it.

While I was aware of numerous harnesses on the market, my personal experience with them was that few effectively worked to truly stop your dog from pulling, those that did work were not biomechanically correct for the dog and none taught you how to train your dog by teaching you to help them to harness their energy the way that Walk In Sync™ does.

The Science Behind the Walk In Sync™ Design

I realize that traditional training tools have been doing their best to focus and redirect your dog's energy, but unfortunately the way they have been going about it can be painful if not downright harmful to your best friend's throat, neck, spine, esophagus, and muscles. It's interesting how much we love our dogs but how little we have questioned how humane the tools are that we use to train them.

One of the most common things I see with behavioral issues today is the lack of clear, consistent boundaries provided by the human whose mindset tends to be: "Do as I say not as I do." We often ask our dogs to behave but rarely do we check in with ourselves to make sure that we are being the most effective and consistent leaders possible. We tend to have four-second attention spans. If pack leaders acted this way in the wild, there would be total chaos in nature.

What I soon became aware of was a principle in physics that states that the further something goes out on a fulcrum, the more energy you need to use to bring it back. So, if your dog is way out in front of you, you have to use a lot more of your own energy to bring the dog back to you because now you are trying to capture his/her already forward momentum.

By placing the clip at the front of the harness, you are actually getting in front of your dog's energy. When you are in front of your dog's energy without choking them, it is far easier for your dog to hear what you are requesting. Therefore, you are assisting your dog in keeping his/her energy in check so that he/she is coming from a far more balanced and centered place.

There are laws that govern the natural world that we humans just do not comprehend yet. We are accustomed to being overly indulged, being able to have what we want when we want it. In some ways, we are spoiled because we don't have to work so hard for what we get;

often what we receive involves little to no physical work at all. Our thoughts jump from thing to thing; our lifestyles have become disposable; and we don't have a really strong value system of priorities or boundaries.

This has led to our current four-second attention spans where we see the world in snippets. Our minds and bodies have become so disconnected not only within our own systems but it has led to us becoming disconnected from our inner world and from nature. Today most of us have no idea where our center is, who we really are, and how powerful we are.

The problem that this presents in working with our dogs (just like in working with our children) is that dogs (pups and children) require clear, consistent, realistic boundaries or parameters within which to learn about, develop, and cultivate their greatest potential. When dogs (and children) are given a safe, consistent ways to test boundaries, they develop their natural curiosity in a way that is healthy and inquisitive (not rebellious), and can grow at a pace that nurtures their best qualities. This requires adult supervision free of past projections of fear, doubt, worry, guilt, blame, resentment, hostility, jealousy, unhealed emotional traumas, anger, and unbalanced male/female energy. It also requires being fully present to the being in front of us with the situation occurring at the moment and keeping our emotions and reactions in check in order to be crystal clear with our responses.

How many of us reading this book would qualify for the second part? I know I certainly would not. But what I have discovered through my experiences with using the Walk In Sync™ Tools and the Ins Sync™ Training Method is that it has vastly improved my ability to make a new choice to be fully present and to be clear when I want to react from a past space that is clouding the truth of the present moment with the dog I am currently working with.

It is this presence that our dogs and our children and our spouses and our lives demand of us. And I have found a highly beneficial, almost imperceptible gateway into this state of presence through the use of the Walk In Sync™ System and Methods.

Walk In Sync™ Philosophy

The philosophy behind the Walk In Sync™ Humane Dog Walking and Training System is simple: Harness your dog's energy to unleash his/her greatest potential and do so in the safest, clearest, most consistent, and humane way possible.

The Walk In Sync™ training tools were designed with the greatest care and love for dogs. The harness is so comfortable and bio-mechanically correct it will not hinder your dog's natural stride. It also allows you to train your dog to back off of pressure by clipping the leash at the front. This versatile harness transforms into a walking harness simply by clipping the leash at the back.

The Accu-Grip leash is exceptional in its versatile design. Two non-slip handles instill confidence and consistency in you, while creating the perfect amount of leash length to give your dog before he/she bumps up against the end of the leash, creating a pressure at his/her chest. When your dog does bump up against the pressure, you simply stand still and do not allow him/her to drag you forward; your dog will be the one to choose to move off of pressure and back off his/her own energy. This lowered state-of-mind energy is most desired for your dog and is what many trainers hope to attain by exercising your dog. The Walk In Sync™ System will get you and your dog there in three easy steps without wear and tear on joints or having to cause pain or harm to their neck by choking him/her into submission.

It is my deepest belief that every dog deserves respectful tools that will keep their body safe while learning what you need from them.

From Walking Your Dog to Transforming the World

6 Secrets Your Dog Wants to Teach You to Unleash Your Greatest Potential

I know that this may sound like a far reach but bear with me for a few moments and you may realize that I am not reaching so far.

When I began developing my Walk In Sync 3 Easy Steps, I would wrap the leash around the dog's chest. It was instantly noticeable to the dog's parents and me how quickly the dog would lower his/her own energy and stop pulling. It was like witnessing a miracle unfolding before our eyes. In seconds, dogs would go from pulling me down the street on a regular collar and leash with me holding on tight, to being under my total control in 30 seconds while I used only my fingertips.

Years ago I had read one of Linda Tellington Jones' books on dogs. Linda is a brilliant woman who invented T-Touch and trains people all around the world in this safe, highly effective method of bodywork that instills light back into our cells and allows our animals bodies to heal rapidly and safely.

In her book, Linda suggested that dogs on collars and choke chains often become disconnected from their bodies which may be a reason why they are less sensitive to listening to their cues from the collar. To remedy this and reconnect the dog with its innate sensitivity and listening skills she shared a leash wrapping technique to assist the dog. I went out with Barney one day and tried it. I took the leash and wrapped it around the perimeter of Barney's entire body from chest to tail. While I don't think I was able to master Linda's technique exactly, I did notice one incredible shift. With the leash around Barney's chest and at front leg height Barney would not walk forward until I did. He was actually looking up at me for the first time ever to ask me what we were doing rather than dragging me around. Although it was not comfortable to be able to walk him with the leash wrapped all the way around him in the way that I interpreted it, this situation provided me with the awareness that a dog that is connected to its whole body is better able to hear you than one whose neck has been repeatedly yanked on.

As I repeated this technique of leash wrapping and developed my own version with dogs of all ages, sizes, breeds, and backgrounds, I was astonished to notice that every dog was aware that pressure at the front of his/her chest meant to back off pulling. This happened more than 100 times, leading me to believe that the reason dogs pull is not due to a failure on their parents' part or the dogs' ignorance but rather on the poor design of traditional training equipment, most of which actually encourages pulling by placing pressure in the wrong place.

I must note here that I am not a big follower of science and scientific studies. I am a huge believer in experiential and observational research. So for those out there that like to have science as the ultimate proof, I cannot claim to know if my above experiment was operant or classical conditioning training. I was not conditioning the dog to get accustomed to the leash around his/her chest, I simply wondered if it would work and tried it spontaneously on lots of different dogs and the results were 100 percent repeatable and consistent.

What I observe from people allowing their dogs to lead the walk is the following:

- Dogs who pull have been taught that pulling is how you move your person forward since they get rewarded each time you move forward.

- Dogs who pull have been allowed to get away with this behavior.

- Dogs who pull are not often true alpha dogs. It's generally the opposite: they are fearful underneath, which could easily lead to aggressive behaviors.

- People who allow their dogs to walk them generally lack clear boundaries in some area of their lives. They allow more than just their dogs to direct their lives.

- Dogs who pull are actually anxious and it is not in their best interests to allow them to lead the walk.

- People who let their dogs lead the walk are generally not wanting to take charge in some area of their lives.

- Flexi leads during training will usually not lead to a well-mannered dog with clear, reliable boundaries.

- People who allow their dogs to lead the walk and have had an aggression incident become more fearful and anxious on walks, thus increasing the dogs' fearfulness and anxiety. Believe me, you do not want a fearful, anxious dog leading your walk.

When I was given the vision for Walk In Sync™ one of the things that was most exciting was the realization that not only would the dogs learn healthy boundaries but so would the people. By utilizing the Accu-Grip™ handles on the leash, I have created a system that puts humans at ease. Now they know exactly where to put their hands in order to provide a clear, solid boundary. They know that the increased security they have to stop the dog using the handles creates a level of confidence that travels down the leash, calming their dogs.

I have observed dozens of humans transforming their habits and shoring up their lazy boundaries instantly with the realization that they have a good grip on their dogs and that their dogs will back off of pressure if they just stand still. Once it dawns on humans that they are actually leading the walk and that their dogs are following their lead, there is a palpable energy shift in people's posture, brainwaves, and attitude. They stand taller, walk with greater authority, and recognize that they have boundaries and that they can call those boundaries when they are being violated. Subsequently there is a noticeable shift in their dogs almost instantly.

Now I may be reaching here, but once you assist people in actually feeling and physiologically experiencing how their boundaries have been overstepped and provide them with the opportunity to step into healthy boundaries with their dogs, the sky is the limit in being able to overcome old habits or limitations where they would let their dogs (and life) drag them around and violate their personal limits.

I have repeatedly observed that once you assist people in reclaiming their internal power and the choices they have to keep choosing and reclaiming that power, you have set them free to be the true light and force they are in the world. When more and more people choose to be their true light and force, the world raises its collective vibration and transforms into a more conscious reality for all.

A New Way: Harness Your Energy to Unleash Your Greatest Potential

I began my career as a Fitness Trainer in 1992. In my years leading up to being a Fitness Trainer I learned one of the most important lessons of my life, discipline and focus are what brings you to where you want to be. I don't mean the kind of discipline like: "go to your room, you are being punished." I mean the kind of discipline and focus that includes a daily practice of getting better at and mastering whatever it is you set out to do. Professional athletes are masters of self-discipline.

In 1994, I had the good fortune of being introduced to my Acupuncturist and future Qi Gong teacher, Dr. Nan Lu. I began studying the ancient Chinese self-healing are of Qi Gong in 1995. Qi Gong is a series of simple movements that when performed on a daily basis assists the body in realigning the energies of the mind, body and spirit so that one is able to more easily and fluidly flow in their lives.

Qi Gong became a healthy discipline in my life. I say healthy because the more I practiced it, the healthier and happier I felt. It became a very positive way to learn how to channel and harness my energy and use it in the most efficient and creative ways to unleash my potential.

As I would partake in my daily Qi practice I began to notice an odd phenomenon occurring. My two dogs would get up from wherever they were in the house and either lay right outside my bedroom door or come into my bedroom and sleep while I practiced.

Eventually I began to put two and two together and realized that the dogs were somehow attuned to the Qi energy and must have liked to soak it up and come join me.

It was from this observation of my dogs choosing to be in the Qi Gong energy that I began to wonder while training if other dogs were aware of this energy and if the dogs would respond to the gentle consistent boundaries that I was holding with them while training. I began by talking less to them and moving them around in silence adjusting what I needed to with them in silence. What I noticed immediately was that the quieter I was with my voice and the more consistent I was with my actions that the dogs responded far better than I could have ever imagined. I was literally walking my talk not talking my walk.

In this new silent state I realized that all I had to do was take action and use the correct tools to teach my dogs how to harness their energy and as a result they were unleashing their greatest potential with ease, simplicity and joy.

I believe that each being on this planet is born with unique skills, gifts, talents and abilities. These come with our initial software package when we are born and it is up to each of us to allow our intuition to guide us to find the best way to harness them and unleash them to reach our greatest potential, whether you are a 2 or 4 legged being.

This is the magic of Walk In Sync™ System and Method, it will assist you in harnessing your dog's energy as well as your own to unleash your greatest potentials.

The In Sync™ Method of Training is Born

As I continued observing the changes in the dogs I was working with, using the Walk In Sync™ tools along with my natural Qi (life force energy) I began to notice that dogs respond more to our energy than they do to our words or treats. I noticed that as I became more self- assured in my role as the natural leader and simply embodied that energy the dogs responded more because they chose to instead of being bribed with food. While I will at times use treats for the introduction of a new behavior or a high distraction situation, I quickly phase out offering treats as a means of getting my dogs to pay attention to me as a crutch because most dogs will work for food but this is not the way of an authentic relationship based on respecting energy. While consciously I thought that this would have the adverse effect of them not paying as much attention I noticed that they paid more attention because they could sense that I was embodying the energy of what I said.

What I became aware of was as my confidence as an Authentic Leader rose so did my dog's willingness to cooperate with me just because they chose to.

I also began to notice that I was continuing to repeat the same 6 Secrets to my clients that seem to be universal to all dogs. As I proceeded with sharing these 6 Secrets I was struck by their simplicity, consistency and effectiveness. What I was in awe of was the change in my human clients as they embodied these Secrets and the rapid change in the dogs as a result of their humans shifting.

What makes the In Sync™ Method unique is that it's based on 6 natural secrets that all dogs know and respect. The first thing you must understand is that being In Sync™ with your dog actually starts within you first. So many training systems teach you the techniques to teach your dog how to sit, stay, come, lay down, etc. And these are all primary skills you must know to properly raise your pup to be a well-mannered dog. And in addition, there are 6 secrets of conduct that once you learn them will not only transform your relationship with your dog it will transform every area of your life.

I learned a long time ago that although I thought I was training dog's they were actually training me. As I began to give up my need for control over them, I started to be in relationship with them. And that relationship has been evolving over the last 18 years to the point that I more clearly understand my role as an Authentic Leader. It is this relationship that is the foundation of my life and the natural affinity I share with these incredible creatures who are so honest, authentic, caring, challenging and have taught me to Walk In Sync with them.

What you will find in this book is:

- Honesty

- Encouragement

- Commitment

- Dedication

- Insights into the Canine Mind

- Insights into Your Own Mind

- A way of being with dogs that begins within you first

- A clear set of rules that every dog knows

- A new way of being and showing up as you in the world

- Clarity of what your dog really thinks

- A simple solution to dog parenting

- Many examples of Walking In Sync together

The In Sync™ Method is an inside out training approach geared towards training you to be an Authentic Leader using the 6 Secrets. Please feel free to apply these secrets liberally as you learn them not only with your dog but with all people and situations in your life.

"A dog is the only thing on earth that loves you
more than you love yourself."
Josh Billings

Secret # 1:
Consistency Is Key

Consistency, Consistency, Consistency

Every retailer knows that the number one key to any successful business is: location, location, location. The number one secret to successful dog training is: consistency, consistency, consistency.

What most proud new puppy parents don't always understand is that once they bring their precious new family member home is that mother dogs train and shape their puppies behavior 24/7. As new puppy parents we have been told that "official training" should start around 16 weeks of age after all the puppies shots have been given. The problem occurs when the puppy goes several days and then weeks if not months without proper and consistent training and clear boundaries at the most critical learning stages that his or her birth mother and puppy siblings would provide round the clock.

Dogs tend to function in an instinctual world, while humans tend to function in more of an emotional and psychological world with instincts almost as an afterthought. Dogs function in packs by instinctively realizing that there is a leader to follow. This follow-the-leader mentality has allowed dogs to survive for thousands of years. Nature, not humans designed this survival technique and I for one think She knows far better than we do the best ways for things to work.

So your new puppy instinctually knows that either you are in change or he/she is in charge. As humans, we unfortunately don't always understand how to communicate in our puppy's language the way his or her mother would. She would be training her puppy from a survival mindset. However, we train our puppy from an emotional/comfort human mindset. That mindset may work (at least most of the time) for our children but it rarely works for our puppies. The reason is that in survival mindset, a mother dog focuses on nipping in the bud those behaviors that would endanger the pup's life in the wild. These behaviors include lack of focus and distraction, laziness or slowing down the rest of the pack, knowing when it's play time and when it's work time. Unlike humans, a dog mother is not interested or vested emotionally in whether or not her pups like her; instead she is concentrating her total attention on ensuring her pup's survival to the best of her abilities.

As a pack animal, who would live in the wild if we had not domesticated dogs 14,000 years ago, your adorable puppy would exhibit behaviors more wolf like than doglike. And your pup would stay with his or her birth mother for up to two years before setting out on his/her own. That's how long it would take a mother dog to prepare her pup to survive and thrive in the wild.

We humans focus on nourishing, nurturing, and teaching our new pup how to fit into our family, which is so completely unnatural to him or her. All the while we are coming from an emotional mindset of pleasing our puppy so that he or she will love us. We do this by setting and breaking our own boundaries all the time; we are inconsistent and this is where our puppy's behavioral issues stem from. Honestly, it is also the same place that our kids' bad behaviors stem from.

The truth is that a mother dog does not care about pleasing her puppies; what she does care about is enforcing acceptable behaviors that will allow her puppies to thrive and correcting unacceptable behaviors that will place her puppies in danger. She has no problem and no guilt whatsoever about correcting her puppies with very clear, consistent boundaries from the beginning so that they don't exhibit that behavior again.

I don't know if you have ever witnessed a mom dog correcting her puppy but sometimes I shirk away from the intensity of the energy she uses to correct. When a mom corrects her pup on a behavior that is dangerous she can go in so fast, so harsh, and so powerfully that the pup is left screaming and in hysterics. At times it's a little scary, seeing how she corrects with the speed and force of lightening, often by grabbing the pup at the side of his throat or around his mouth. Yet it is never emotional, nor personal. The mother's correction is clear, exacting to that specific behavior, and shocking enough to the puppies that they learn very quickly to never do it again...or at least to think twice before they do. She corrects quickly to adjust an excessive or deficient energy or any personality imbalances she detects in the puppies so that they become aware of their place in the pack.

Interestingly, when women act this assertively and clearly like a momma dog they are called bitches, but when men exhibit this behavior they are called leaders or bosses.

Considering how different human and dog languages are, it is interesting to me that we do not spend more time understanding dog language to properly and more effectively communicate with our dogs. Rarely do we take the time to understand or learn our pup's language to be more consistent with him from the moment he comes home.

My biggest frustration in training is the lack of consistency that my clients show when working with their dogs. In our crazy hustle and bustle world, we have little consistency in our own lives, which might explain why so many kids have ADD/ADHD and dog bites and aggression are on the upswing. How can we be consistent and present in our dogs' lives, especially in training, when we are so scattered in our own?

When I speak with my clients about training I emphasize the fact that training is not something you do for an hour a day, like watching the nightly news or your favorite TV show. Training is a way of life. It's setting clear boundaries that this is how we work, these are the rules, and we follow them. As your pups mature they will gain more freedom if you have built a solid, clear foundation with them and can trust them and they can trust you as a consistent leader.

When I first start working with new clients, the major fear that I have heard over and over is that training will take up too much of their time, which is already in short supply. By the end of our first training session, my clients are so relieved when I ask of them only five minutes maximum, four to five times a day to work with their pup or dog. I have received many strange looks when my clients hear the words "maximum five minutes." They seem uncertain, and wonder whether I am lying to them or they have misheard me.

I am sure most of you are familiar with repetition. I am actually not talking about the boring old- style way of training that involved a straight hour of doing the same thing over and over again. The dog got bored; the person got bored. This type of training was draining.

What I am talking about is something that happens when you become aware of how smart your dog is and how quickly he or she can learn. The biggest difference between repetition and consistency is that repetition is not always about setting clear boundaries while consistency is about always setting clear boundaries. And if you stay consistent with your dog about what is permissible and what is not in a calm, authentic manner, your dog will understand your clarity and not test your boundaries for long. (I just heard a huge sigh of relief from many parents reading this who are going to practice this with their kids.)

Authentic Leadership

I have a term I like to use that replaces the "alpha" term, which I call Authentic Leadership. Consistency in terms of Authentic Leadership is about learning and living a certain energy or quality of being that is infused in and through everything you do. It's like practicing yoga or Tai Chi. Eventually you become one with the energy of yoga or Tai Chi. Repetition is like going to yoga or Tai Chi class to practice it, but once you leave class you resume your regular life. In repetition alone, you never truly achieve the oneness with the thing you are practicing because you are not applying it to all areas of your life. You participate in the act of it but you rarely become one with it.

Authentic Leadership is about being the embodiment of a consistent, clear leader who masters the art of redirecting energy to allow it to flow in the easiest manner. At times it is calm and quiet. At times it may need to momentarily roar like a lion to correct a specific behavior and then it immediately returns back to calmness and clarity. Authentic Leadership is never personal; it is always present and clear in the moment. It does not carry anger, disappointment, or grudges with it into the future. It does what it needs to in the moment and then returns to the peace of moment. It is not about dominating dogs or puppies, or throwing anger at them or making them feel bad about themselves; it only corrects and reshapes the behavior. Authentic Leadership carries no judgment within it.

In other words, when you teach your dog new things to master for not more than five minutes at a time, and then stay consistent with the yes's and no's, you are teaching your dog all day long. Set your routine with the puppy, the same way every day so that he/she can count on your consistency and leadership while playing within those boundaries. As they get older, you can change up the routines but still remain consistent with your yes's and no's. Then, no matter where you go or what you do together, the essence of your relationship is built on your Authentic Leadership skills and your dog will trust you in any situation and you can trust your dog in any situation. If you do this, it won't even seem like you are training at all, instead it will seem like this is simply the natural way you live your lives.

The easiest way I teach my clients to master this is by four or five or more five-minute training sessions. Short, sweet, and to the point. Then during the day I may have them incorporate the lessons from their mini-sessions into a walk. So let's say they are teaching sit and stay. I have them do their mini-sessions and then when they go out on a walk, I have them incorporate the sit and stay at different times during the walk. This way we break down the specifics for the dog, then make it part of their normal routine. By working in this manner, there is a sense of flow and continuity that sets the pair up for success.

A True Leader Is Consistent

When I think of Authentic leaders in humanity, people like Gandhi, the Dalai Lama, John F. Kennedy, Jr., and Martin Luther King, Jr. spring to mind. To me, what made each of them leaders is the consistency of their message along with them walking their talk. For Gandhi, the message was "if you want to change the world it begins with you and that there is always a peaceful solution to all problems." For The Dalai Lama it is "compassion for all beings." For John F. Kennedy Jr., it was, "ask not what your country can do for you but what you can do for your country." And for Dr. King, Jr., it was "all people are created equal and have the same inalienable rights to the pursuit of life, liberty, and freedom."

When I think of groups of people who are authentic leaders, I think of the Native American cultures that had lived peaceably among each other for hundreds if not thousands of years. That is not to say that there were never any disagreements on territory or other issues but how they handled the situations were within the context of the disagreement. An out-and-out war was never started to launch a massive attack against another tribe. (Interesting to note too that while dogs are territorial animals, they would never start a war.)

Their leadership focused on their culture as part of a large whole. They were merely another part of the earth, and they honored and respected all life by wasting nothing, thinking about their future in terms of the next seven generations, and respecting the rights and gifts of each member of the tribe. All members were a valuable contribution.

In the dog world, consistency is not only about action, it is about steadiness of one's character. I always say, "Authentic lead dogs are born that way." They have an inner perception that they are leaders, an instinctive inner and outer physical strength brought about by their calmness and knowingness. Although they are often portrayed as the most rambunctious or aggressive of the bunch, this is simply not true. Authentic lead dogs have to learn the rules and grow like any other member of the pack, but the difference is that they have an innate ability to lead and it gives them a certain sense of confidence and peace in realizing that the other members will rely on their quiet knowing as well as their brute strengths.

Many people mislabel their dogs as "alphas" after watching them trying to take immediate control of situations and dominate other dogs. This is not an Authentic Leader. Almost every dog I have worked with expressing these "alpha" behaviors is hiding his or her fearful nature behind this show of brawn. When I stop these dogs in their tracks and divert them from exhibiting aggression, most of them begin to shake, their eyes get shifty, and the underlying lack of self-confidence shows itself. Many then begin whining like little puppies annoyed at not getting their way. I point this out as many cases of attacks are mislabeled as aggression when they are actually fear based.

It is really important to know the difference between the two so that you can address the issue properly. You do not want to dominate a fearful dog acting aggressively; you actually want to shore up your leadership skills in your daily work so that the dog can relax and trust that you will be his or her leader. You want to build that dog's confidence. You can do this by teaching him or her to lower his or her energy by boosting up your own Authentic Leadership energy.

Leadership is a funny thing. There are all different kinds of leaders who range from the Dalai Lama to Hitler. In my awareness, a true leader helps his or her people see the power that lies within them to accomplish their goals while letting the people take the credit. There are leaders who do get caught up in their own egos based on narcissism and who become the kind of leader who usurps or limits peoples' control over their own lives through domination and often fear. And then there are leaders who uplift and inspire people to bring out the best in themselves knowing that the stronger each individual is, the stronger the whole will be. Leaders of this caliber use their abilities to consistently remind others of their own true worth and value leading to the fullest expression of each individual.

If you truly want to practice your Authentic Leadership skills, become a good leader to your dog. Be consistent and be the kind of human your dog would want to follow. Pay attention to your body language. Stand tall, relax, and breathe full. Find and cultivate your sense of peace within yourself and know yourself so that when you ask your dog to follow your lead, he or she feels safe and knows what you expect, and understands how to meet your requests. When your dog has done a good job, praise him or her, and above all don't make or take things personally. Lead with confidence and clarity in the path you have chosen for your life. Be clear but also be willing to be soft and vulnerable, and yield when necessary. But most of all be consistent.

Consistency Creates Trust

One thing I began to realize in training was that when I was consistent and clear in my requests and boundaries with my dogs, my dogs had far fewer behavioral issues, they tested my boundaries far less, and our relationship was much more peaceful.

When training my chocolate lab Barney years ago, I realized that there was one thing he could consistently count on me for: I would always take it personally when he did not listen, like when he completely ignored my existence by dragging me behind him or he refused to come when called. As a fitness trainer at the time, I was learning how to develop and apply consistency in my training but had no idea back them how to apply the same consistency, calmness, and clarity with my dog.

This led to a lot of frustration on both of our parts as I had been taught to do the repetition thing, which took a lot of time and left both Barney and I more disconnected in our relationship than anything else. I had no idea how to be patient with him and every time he didn't do what I asked I went further into frustration and angst, signaling to Barney that I was not a leader he could trust. It took me years to learn how important building trust with a dog is to the foundation of the relationship (to any relationship). This is why when I developed the In Sync™ Method I knew it was one of the first things I needed to share with dog guardians because if you start with this at the beginning, you are able to build a rock solid foundation and partnership with your dog that will last a lifetime. And what I have found through training and rebuilding broken foundations with dogs is that no matter what age, no matter what breed, no matter what kind of issue or abuse the dog has gone through, the #1 secret is always in your hands and that is consistency on your part will assist in transforming that dog's behavior more than anything else.

Over the years, I have come to see that consistency is a key to building trust: trust in our relationship with our dogs, with our spouses and children, with our world. When I request that my dogs do something, all it takes is one look in my eyes for them to know that they can trust what I am asking of them because I have been a consistent leader who has kept them safe. They realize that they can rely on me. It also only takes one look for them to realize that I meant what I said. Because we have built upon consistency to create this trust, it goes both ways. I can trust them and give them far greater freedom on walks and in the things we get to do together.

In terms of human relationships, it has been my experience that when we are consistent people trust us more; we are generally given far more responsibility because we have been consistent and others can count on us. Personally, it feels great to be consistent with yourself and know that you can trust yourself.

Consistency Builds Confidence

Consistency also builds confidence in ourselves and others. When we apply consistency to anything in our lives, we develop a level of confidence as a result of the skills we develop. When I was a fitness trainer and working on developing my own muscle strength and body, there was a direct correlation between the consistency I applied to my training and the confidence I had in my own body and physical abilities. I noticed the very same thing in my clients who began transcending many of their own limitations—as they gained strength on the outside, they also gained it on the inside.

When we apply our dog training skills consistently on an everyday basis, we also build a level of confidence in ourselves as we watch our dogs listening and responding in positive ways to what we are requesting. In turn, our dogs build confidence in us as their leaders and in themselves as members of our family by the consistency we apply.

Love = Respect

In a dog's world there is a difference between love and respect. In your dog's world respect is one of the highest forms of love. In our human world we have various meanings and interpretations for love, and very few of those actually are based on respect. Our human love frequently is based on the unhealed, unspoken, unacknowledged, unconscious, and unmet emotional needs that we are trying to get met through other people. Our love is often times self-focused and based around ourselves. Our dogs' sense of love is around the pack first.

When I am consistent with my boss, my friends, and my loved ones, they begin to develop a level of confidence in me knowing that I will be there for them when they need me. I also develop a level of confidence in myself that I can be there for them when they need me.

A Solid Foundation Requires Consistency

In order to have a solid relationship with you puppy or dog, consistency is the key to apply with them each and every day. This will be the basis for your foundation with your dog.

Over the years I have found it is far easier, although it takes more daily discipline and awareness on your part, to be consistent from the beginning as you start to build a solid foundation and avoid cracks that could appear later. It is far easier to educate your new pup about boundaries and stay consistent with him or her from the beginning than it is to try and wrestle with him or her later or turn to using harsher training tools when your dog is far more vested in his or her behaviors, he or she is much larger, and you are frustrated.

Dogs Require:

- **Consistency**
- **Clear Boundaries**
- **Routine**
- **Clear, Respectful Leadership**

I cannot tell you how many parents I have worked with while training that have asked me if this would work with their kids. Not to compare your children to dogs at all, but if you were to apply the same clarity and consistency in your boundaries, not taking anything personally or making it about an unhealed emotional issue you are dealing with, you and your children you will attain far greater peace and results.

Let Go of the Story

One of the key things I share with all of my clients who bring home rescue dogs is to start out being a consistent leader from the beginning. The dog has already been traumatized and so his or her level of trust has been broken somewhere. Do not feel bad for the dog and project your human emotions on him or her or you will further ingrain in your dog's emotional behavior. In the dog world it's about survival, so if you had a trauma you get over it, get back in the present, and get fully engaged in the now. Dogs don't feel sorry for themselves. They either remain attached to the trauma by post-traumatic stress disorder, which is often seen in unpredictable behaviors, or they move on. And note in wild dogs (like wolves) there is very little discovery of post-traumatic stress.

When humans take home a rescue dog, they tend to reinforce the fear, abandonment, trauma, or unstable behavior the dog is exhibiting by catering to that behavior, and humanizing that behavior, and continuing to perpetuate the story of that dog's trauma by sharing it with anyone who will listen over and over again. If you're guilty of this, stop immediately, get into the present moment with your dog, and be here now. This type of reinforcement can actually promote the growth of that negative behavior or at least keep it intact for a long time. Clients will tell me the dog's story to explain his behaviors and when I ask how long they have had the dog, they'll reply, "seven years."

Sara and Sam: A Client's Story

This actually happened with a client I will call Sara and her rescue Jack Russell, Sam. Sara called me because Sam had this nervous habit of lunging at children then running behind her to hide. I asked her when he developed the habit and she told me it was about the time she rescued him. I asked Sara what she had done to correct it. She said in the beginning she felt bad for him because he had been in a home with two little boys who teased him a lot. She didn't want to correct him because he had been through trauma. So when the behavior would happen, Sara would let Sam hide behind her and tell him in a calm soothing voice that everything was okay.

I observed the behavior in action when we had one of Sara's little neighbors come over. All of a sudden it occurred to me to ask Sara how long ago she had rescued Sam. She said, "Eight years ago." That was the first time I really saw how much we humans can keep our dogs locked into a pattern of post-traumatic stress patterns.

Sara and I talked about two things. First, regardless of what happened to Sam in his past, we agreed that this behavior was no longer acceptable. Now Sara had to be Sam's leader and step up to the plate to correct him when this occurred. I demonstrated to her how to redirect and, when needed, block Sam's energy from extending outward to the child and to how to refocus him on her leadership as she stood right in front of him. It was truly amazing to witness how quickly Sam learned a new way to be with kids once Sara stopped feeling bad for him. She helped him shift that energy of fear back to one of confidence in trusting now that she had stepped into her leadership shoes.

Second, we talked about a "human phenomena" I witness all the time and have participated in many times as well.

We talked about the stories humans hold onto about past traumas and the tendency we have to be triggered by the past, which distracts us from living within the moment. This is a really important concept to grasp because in every moment we have the choice to react from the past or respond from the present. When we discipline ourselves and our dogs to stay in the present moment and respond to each present moment it allows us to leave our past where it needs to be left, behind us. When we try to respond in the present but are reacting from the past, we are not fully present for ourselves and our dogs. This is why most dogs or pups will second-guess you and not listen when they cannot sense your full presence.

After eight years of being together, Sam was no longer a "rescue dog," he was Sara's dog. Sara was keeping up Sam's rescue story, for perhaps a multitude of reasons; none of them were helping little Sam though. So by assisting Sara in becoming aware of how she had been holding onto Sam's past story, a light bulb went off in Sara's head making her aware that this pattern was not just with Sam but part of her story as well. Once she made the connection about holding onto past stories and making excuses, it facilitated Sara in letting and choosing to be the leader she needed to be to Sam.

Both Sara and Sam are doing exceptionally well and thriving in their new roles. Sam also really likes kids now that he knows he can safely interact with them in a confident manner like Sara taught him.

Your Authentic Leadership is the most important thing you can give your dog.

Personal Story: Indie, the Dog Who Rescued Me

I had been scanning the rescue section of the newspaper for a small female dog for about two months. One of the local rescues in the Aspen Valley had advertised a female mini dachshund who needed a new home. After several weeks of trying to decipher whether this dog was actually available for adoption, a dear friend who operates a local kennel and cares for rescued dogs at her facility called me about a male dachshund who had just come to her. She suggested I come up and take a look.

When Indie and I met we were both a bit tentative. I never had a small dog and he had just had some pretty bad experiences. My girlfriend suggested I take him home for the night and see how it went. I did and at the five-day marker, I knew he was meant to be with me.

Indie and I developed a close relationship pretty quickly. Early on I assessed that due to his abandonment and then being placed in a home that did not truly understand the breed and that was experiencing its own turmoil, Indie would need some retraining and a very clear and consistent leader.

During our early time, I asked Indie about his experiences. He shared with me how he had been abandoned at four months and just left by the side of the river. He also shared how he had been hit on his rump for going to the bathroom in the house, as well as not really having anyone to bond with. As our time together and training progressed and Indie became more confident, loving, and sweet, people would remark at what a nice Dachshund he was. I would, in turn, share his distressing background and with each comment, perpetuate his story while remarking how far he had come. Looking back in some way I think I was looking to validate myself for having done a good job with him.

About a year and a half later (sometimes I am a little slow to catch on) as we were walking in the park, we met another dog parent who had mentioned that he had Dachshunds as a kid and that they were so mean. He was very impressed with how nice Indie was. Just as I was about to tell one more story about Indie's background, I stopped myself dead in my tracks as I realized that Indie was over his past, he didn't need it told anymore, so why was I continuing to tell it. At that moment, he looked directly at me and me at him and there was a mutual feeling of freeing ourselves from the past and living our lives now in the present.

I responded to the gentleman by saying, "Thank you for noticing. Indie is a really amazing being and he loves having a clear, confident leader in me who respects his independence but is ultimately in charge. He has done really well with his training."

From that day on I shared this awareness with every dog rescue parent. It has been a true turning point in their relationship. Dogs don't hold onto the past if they are in a pack situation because their life demands that they be in the present. So they are masters of being present. When we rescue a dog and hear their story and we repeat it, we keep them locked into that past state, which is not where you want your dog to be. You want your dog's full presence and your full presence to live here now and enable you both to walk in sync.

Stay Present

It's interesting to look at how vested we are as a society in our dramas and how we love to keep repeating them, even if they are someone else's. And it's interesting how when you stick to the present moment and give short precise answers, people often view you as rude or curt because there is no story to feed off of or identify with.

What any dog needs is a clear, confident, consistent leader who that dog can trust and therefore realize it is okay to let go of old issues. This is the quickest way back to a sound mind and balanced behavior for the dog (and also for any human) and the building of a new solid foundation. You don't just want to fill in the cracks, you want to lay a new foundation that is rock-solid.

I always recommend re-training rescue dogs. For me it does not matter if the dog knows every command in the book and can cook you breakfast and serve it to you in bed. What matters is the bond that you and the dog will develop as a result of consistent daily work together. This bond must be established between the two of you so that you can learn to mutually trust and have total confidence in one another. Once that occurs, you will walk in sync being the amazing team you were destined to be.

The Bond

Clear, consistent, authentic leadership is the behavior that creates "the bond" we truly wish to share with our dogs. When we apply this leadership properly, it is not only effective at keeping us safe, it is equally effective in deepening the bonds of our relationship with our dog. I believe that it is this unbreakable bond that is at the heart of what all of us truly wish to share with our animal companions.

Dr. Allen Schoen writes extensively about the value and significance of this bond in his book, *Kindred Spirits: How the Remarkable Bond Between Humans and Animals Can Change the Way We Live*. *Kindred Spirits* details the many ways in which the human-animal bond can provide a wellspring of love and support, and help us all lead happier, healthier, and more fulfilling lives.

I had the great honor and pleasure of meeting Dr. Allen Schoen for a retreat weekend. Dr. Schoen is one of those rare and precious individuals who speaks and walks his path in grace and beauty. He and I share a great love, respect, and honoring of nature, the wisdom of the animal kingdom, and the desire to serve animals and their humans in the highest way possible.

During our time together there was a discernible energy Dr. Schoen emitted that was palpable from our first hello. There is a oneness with all life that he embodies and has captured in his books as he actually lives that bond with every two-legged or four- legged being he meets. It is that bond that allows the true richness of our relationships with our dogs to develop and allows us as humans to unleash the true greatness and wholeness within ourselves.

Although I instruct humans and animals how to navigate the world of getting along and listening to what each needs, one of the most fulfilling aspects of my job is when the human/ animal instructional relationship transforms into the human/animal partnership relationship. It touches my heart deeply each time I see levels of trust building and forming where walls once existed. When that happens, kindness, caring, mutual admiration, and adoration replace fear, doubt, and insecurity. Clear communication and ease replace nervousness, agitation, and control.

While I am not advocating the leadership position to be a totally equal one, I am aware of when the relationship transforms to a place of being open and willing to learn from each other. That is where the true bond between dog and human creates expansion and such great joy in people and pooches.

Take time sometimes to step back and see the world from your dog's perspective and allow yourself to be aware of what you are learning from your dog as well. You will gain massive amounts of respect for the intelligence of your dog. And in a dog's world respect = love.

"Sometimes you panic and find yourself emitting remarks so profoundly insane that you would be embarrassed to say them to your dog. Your dog would look at you and think to itself, "I may lick myself in public, but I'd never say anything as stupid as that."
Dave Barry

Secret # 2:

Say What You Mean
and Mean What You Say

Saying what you mean and meaning what you say is the second step in building a solid foundation and learning to walk in sync with your dog.

If I request my dog to sit, I will not move until I get a sit from my dog, even if I have to use a gentle correction. If I say *sit* and then I allow my dog to get away with not sitting, I have given my dog a completely mixed message. He instinctively knows that I am not honoring my word. Therefore, he will be less likely to listen to me or will test me many times before he listens.

In our relationship with our puppy or dog it is vital that we be people of our word. Our word is our honor. It is the one thing that our puppy or dog will realize in half a second if we mean business or not. And although we think we mean business, if we aren't committed to our word our four-legged friends bust us even before we realize it.

Our animals read our energy. They sense the actualization of our intentions and the energy we have committed to following through on our word. Animals know if we will follow through even before we do.

The vital thing is that we say what we mean and mean what we say. If I call my dog on a come, I don't mean in few minutes or on my dog's time. I mean now. And if it's not now then I need to be willing to follow up on what I asked for with a correction to let my dog know I meant what I said. Once this is established, I have a dog who is willing to take my command and give me what I request on a consistent basis. And the beautiful thing is that I never have to raise my voice, I simply raise my energy because that's the language that is the most natural for my dog to understand. Remember the saying: Actions speak louder than words. If your dog cannot connect with your words, step up your energy and he/she will hear you loud and clear.

Bitches Never Apologize (for a Correction)

If you have ever watched a mother dog correct her puppies, it can be downright scary. After the bitch gives a low guttural growl followed by a quick lashing out, you can hear the high-pitched yelps of her scared-to-death puppies. She corrects quick to adjust an excessive or deficient energy or personality imbalances she detects in the pups so that they know their place in the pack.

But one thing you will never see is that bitch expressing to her puppies how sorry she is. Mother dogs don't apologize. They don't even wait around to see how their puppies are doing or feeling after her correction. The bitch will correct and walk away, leaving a stunned puppy in her aftermath. The puppy who was corrected will then slink back over to his/her mother and begin making amends by licking inside her gums while rolling on his/her back and being cute.

Even with that puppy licking to say how sorry he or she is, Mom will never apologize. She never makes it personal or takes it personally; she just issues the correction, nips the bad habit in the bud, and moves on. Through this detached clarity, her puppy learns quickly and definitively that certain behaviors are just not tolerated and non-negotiable.

Not once does Mom feel bad or guilty for being clear about her correction. This gives her the distinct advantage of not having to repeat herself with continuous corrections. It is generally severe enough that the pup will get over it. Then the pup will learn how to manage his/her energy rather quickly, without backtalk, crocodile tears, or tantrums like many children.

A mother dog is very clear about her boundaries with her pups. Unlike human mothers, you will rarely see a bitch be manipulated by her pups' emotional outbursts. She is in charge: What she says goes and there is no variance. She says what she means and means what she says because she is training for survival. No broken boundaries there.

Personal Experience

As humans, this isn't such a bad characteristic to pick up. I remember the first time I saw this work with my niece. We were walking around Target. She was about three years old and in the cart. She wanted to grab something off a shelf, which she had tried to do two previous times. I had told her to stop. On the third go-round I looked her clear in the eye and said, "NO!" I would not take my energetic gaze and boundary off of her. She then proceeded with some crocodile tears, while I continued to stare at her as if to say, "Hey kid, I am your aunt not your mother and those fake tears don't work with me." She got it really quick and immediately shut those tears off. Soon a smile appeared on her face as she realized the boundary had been set and she couldn't break it. She changed her tune really quickly.

The truth is that a mother dog does not care about

pleasing her puppies; she cares about acceptable and unacceptable behaviors that will allow that pup to thrive or that will get him/her killed. She has no problem and no guilt whatsoever about correcting her puppy with very clear, consistent boundaries from the beginning so that he/she doesn't exhibit that behavior again.

Just considering the fact that human language and dog language are so different it is amazing that we do not spend more time understanding dog language to properly and more effectively communicate with our dogs. Rarely do we take the time to understand or learn our pup's language to be more consistent with them from the moment they come home. I will reveal later the #1 form of communication that dogs use and I can tell you it is not what you are expecting.

Correct the Behavior, Not the Dog

Let's look at the difference here between a clear, clean, unemotional correction and an angry correction. Mom is correcting the behavior, not the pup. She is specifically saying that this behavior is unacceptable, not that this pup is unacceptable. She is unattached to how anyone perceives her clarity; she is simply clear and then over it.

We humans however tend to take things more personally. We allow our anger to get the best of us so we end up correcting the being. We say "bad dog" rather than "no chew" or "poop outside." And on top of not being specific about the bad behavior, we stay offended and mad. As soon as you take something personally your energy will morph and you will have an "emotional ding" in your field. Your animal can sense this and is less likely to listen to and respect you authority until you get back in balance and let that go.

Understand the difference?

Always correct the behavior, not the dog.

Dogs Are Masters of Inner Alignment; Humans Are Learning

Animals are masters of inner energy alignment. Their thoughts, feelings, and emotions are in alignment. Unless there has been a case of abuse or a misalignment of energies due to inconsistent training most dogs are far clearer than their human counterparts.

In the human world it is rare that what we think, feel and say are in alignment. We often think one thing, say something else and feel conflicted about what we are asking for. This confuses our dogs to no end because as energy beings they feel that we are out of alignment within ourselves which makes us an unreliable and unpredictable leader. It also irritates us as humans because we think we are being clear when we are not and then end up frustrated with our dogs when in reality it is us not understanding their language. When working with my clients on a new command with their puppies, I ask my clients to visualize their dogs doing what my clients want. Then I ask my clients to feel confident that their puppies will do it. In this way, I am training my clients to be in energetic alignment with themselves and ultimately with their dogs.

Our dogs can teach us to master our inner alignment, which will serve us quite well in our daily lives. How many times have you said one thing, thought another, and acted completely different from both? As many of us know, this too often leads to confusion and chaos, creating dramas in our lives that are not necessary. Perhaps our dogs are here to teach us the secret of aligning our thoughts, words, and actions.

As a student of the internal healing art of Qi Gong, I spent a lot of time meditating and cultivating the inner energy of my body in order for it to balance and flow to its highest potential. This practice requires a level of presence and letting go that is not found in most of our daily lives. It helps one to develop a clarity of being by stilling the mind of rampant thoughts that keep us preoccupied and unfocused. This stilling of the mind and being fully present is the place that dogs live in 24/7.

When we can attain the level of quiet in our minds like that of our dogs, we are one step closer to truly understanding and being compatible with our dogs in their energy field.

Have you ever tried to see life through your dog's eyes? Have you ever quieted your mind enough to try and hear what he/she hears? Have you ever just followed your dog around to see what he or she does? How can we possibly be humane and healthy leaders to our dogs if we don't even understand them?

A Dog's Strongest Form of Communication

I learned a long time ago that a dog's strongest form of communication is pictures. If you ask your dog to sit while visualizing him/her not sitting, your dog will focus on the picture more than the words. Then clients become frustrated because their dogs don't sit. Clients start approaching their dogs with a frustrated attitude, further reinforcing the incorrect picture. This now intensifies the energy, which does not go over well with puppies. When we switch the picture and align it with the words, dogs quickly understand what we are asking for.

So before you ask your dog for any command, visualize a clear mental picture in your head of what you do want. I am willing to bet you that your results with your dog improve by at least 75 percent.

The way I discovered this was by learning the art of telepathic communication. We are all born with psychic and telepathic abilities. Every single human, as well as all members of the animal and plant kingdoms, can communicate telepathically. Although we often think that animals only communicate using nonverbal body cues or changes in their voices, they communicate telepathically all of the time with one another, sending visual pictures back and forth. Once we humans pierce the veil of disbelief that we can actually telepathically communicate with all other species, an entirely new world and reality is available to us in the nonverbal realms.

Although I have been practicing this for more than 18 years, and have had some absolutely miraculous communications and experiences with animals through telepathic communication, I don't ask you to take my word for it. However, I will ask you to try it for yourself and open the door to another possibility. Use this ancient art of sending and receiving pictures during training and I sense you will have your own phenomenal experiences. (Animal Communication Home Study Course Available—see back of book)

Client Story

I ran into a client of mine who I had not seen in quite awhile. She had since adopted a new Bernese Mountain dog to add to her family of two other canines. She had ordered some coffee and suggested I go out to the car to say hello to the dogs. Her new 10- month-old puppy popped her head up. I could see the puppy's conflict: her excitement mixed with her caution of being a protector of the car. I told her telepathically that it was okay, that I knew her whole family, and that I was familiar to her, it was just that she had not met me yet. Immediately she relaxed and softened knowing I was not a threat.

I went back inside to see my client again, mentioning what had just transpired. Kristen's eyes lit up as I had nailed the puppy's personality. Then she mentioned something that I had taught her and that she had been using for more than eight years. She said, "Alecia, I will never forget when you shared with me that animals' primary form of communication is in pictures. I have used that so many times with all my animals and it really is true, it totally works."

I smiled, glad I could have an impact and glad that it was a key to her work with her animals.

Personal Story—Wolfie and the Coyotes

One summer afternoon I laid down in bed as I was not feeling so well. Outside of my bedroom window, my boyfriend's dog Wolfie sat under the shade of a big pine tree. Wolfie never barks, but at that moment he started barking up a storm. I got up and went to the window to see what was going on. I asked him, telepathically why he was barking. He told me that there was a coyote up on the red rock ridge outside our house. I asked him to let me see through his eyes where the coyote was.

Immediately, my eyes were drawn to the exact spot where the coyote stood, and I saw him with my own eyes. Wolfie then said that there was another coyote up there as well. I didn't believe him for some reason about that second one. I asked him again to show me through his eyes where the coyote was. Sure enough, he took my eyes to exactly where the second one was. I just smiled, half at my own skepticism, half at how cool being able to telepathically communicate with animals is. I thanked Wolfie and told him to keep doing a great job watching over the house.

Your Clarity Gives Everyone Else the Opportunity to Be Clear

When our communication is clear with our dogs, our entire relationship functions in a way that is stress-free, balanced, and harmonious.

How many times have you watched a fearful pet parent chasing his or her dog down the street? The dog could care less, and more than likely was actually running away from the person's frenetic energy. Remember the dog's strongest form of communication is pictures.

How many times have you seen a person frazzled and distressed because his or her dog is not listening? This pet parent is taking it personally because he or she gave the dog more freedom than the dog was ready for.

One of the problems that occurs in the situation of a dog running away is that the person becomes scared. He or she keeps showing the mental picture of the dog running away, thus ramping up the energy because he or she is so fearful. Even though the person wants the dog to come, he or she is screaming at the dog with their pictures in a way that pushes the dog away.

This is not being clear. Being clear is holding the picture in your mind of what you want, not what you don't. In this instance, it is your dog returning to you. You call him or her in a way that projects safety and then your dog calmly returns back to you.

Clarity of knowing what you want is essential to transferring to your dog. If you are calm and clear and know what you want, it becomes very easy for your dog to give you what you desire. Your clarity brings clearness to every situation and to all communications.

The same is true for all situations in your life. Once you are clear about what you want and ask for it, and you are committed to doing whatever it takes to allow what you want to occur, it does. However, if you are allowing limiting beliefs, unchecked old habits or patterns, and expectations to interfere and obscure your clarity underneath it all then you have some work to do on clearing up those inner limitations.

Remember that being willing to be clear, saying what you mean, and meaning what you say is a key to working with your dog and all others in your life.

Honoring Your Word Builds Respect

Your word is you. When you ask your dog for something, you are putting your word out to receive what you would like. If you do not honor your word, your dog will not honor it either.

Your word—good, bad, right, or wrong—is how you honor your dog and yourself. If you yell at your dog, that is how you are honoring yourself. If you hit your dog, that is how you are honoring yourself. If you allow your dog to step all over you and not listen, that is how you are honoring yourself.

When you give and honor your word, you build respect with your dog and yourself. In a dog's world, you are your word and your actions; if you back it up with your actions, you will earn respect.

The same holds true with people. When you give your word and back it up with action, you gain the respect of people and yourself. When you give your word but your actions are not in alignment with your word, you lose the respect of people and yourself.

Violate Your Word and You Violate Yourself (and Others Will Violate You)

If you ask your dog for a particular behavior and you allow him/her to not listen to you, you have just violated yourself and allowed your dog to violate you. Many times I see my clients allowing their requests to be violated. Then they get mad or frustrated at their dogs because they are allowing themselves to be violated and taking it out on their dogs for mirroring back this pattern.

Dogs do not feel like victims; they know they are either safe or not. In our human world, we go around feeling like victims and project victimization on others who have been hurt. We reinforce one another's past stories and essentially band together and enable ourselves to stay victims by association. In the dogs' world, there is no such thing as a victim because dogs do not victimize one another. Dogs are very clear about what behaviors are acceptable and unacceptable in a pack. Victimization does not fall anywhere on the list.

When we violate ourselves and allow others to violate us, we are acting like victims. We will continue to draw attacks to ourselves until we reclaim our wholeness. That is the best thing we can do for our dogs as well. Yes an incident occurred, but it was in the past and now it's up to us to lick our figurative wounds and get back in the game ASAP.

Listening to that Inner Voice Could Save You a Lot of Trouble.

Personal Story

I was called in to work with a client's dog who had an issue with excessive barking. Jake was rescued in another part of Colorado about three years ago. He was a street dog who had been on his own for a while before he was rescued. In his new home, Jake developed food aggression issues. My client, M, rescued him and had a few trainers work with him and said Jake was much better. Now the issue was not being able to get Jake to stop barking at everyone and everything.

My initial instinct with Jake was that he was hiding something and was not a trustworthy dog. So I started by speaking with his human and doing bodywork on Jake to release any tense muscles to see if he was stressed in that way. He was very stressed—for a 40- pound dog he had the most muscle tension I had ever worked on in a dog. We chatted and I worked for about 20 minutes. At that point, Jake was completely relaxed and became part of the floor. I had touched him everywhere and my level of trust in him skyrocketed.

As M and I were talking, his wife came in and M showed her how relaxed Jake was. She sat on the top corner of his living room chair with her arms and legs crossed, rolling her eyes backwards as M shared this, as if to say, "Yeah, heard it before, this dog is kooky and I doubt this lady can do anything." In that instant, inside my head, I heard myself say, "You know what, I don't think this is going to work as it requires everyone being on the same page. I don't feel that you are up for this, so let's just stop here." I heard those words clear as a bell and yet somehow they never spilled off my tongue.

What transpired next was a result of not saying what I meant and meaning what I said. I asked M's wife to show me how the dog listens. She grabbed a cookie and asked him to sit on his bed. He did so the first two times and then he sat, but not on the bed. I asked her if it was okay for me to step in. Then I stepped up the energy just a little so that she would have exactly what she asked for. I took Jake's leash and moved it in an upward direction, then placed my hand on his butt to ask for a sit. The next thing that happened was completely shocking and has never happened to me before. Before I realized, it Jake viciously attacked me, biting me 26 times and sending me into utter shock. A hospital trip was warranted and stitches were applied. The healing process was very painful.

I have been around a lot of dogs over the past 15 years. It has taken me more than 40 years to remember that I need to take my own advice. When my body said this isn't going to work, I should have listened. I broke my own rule and, as a result, ended up with a very painful, scarred, and shocked body.

Now, I could have gone into victim mode; after all, the dog was a previous offender biter. But as soon as I was able, I worked with my friends who are energy healers and we cleared the shock and trauma from my cells. Once that was cleared, I could let go of what happened and resume my life, not as a victim, but as a person responsible for all my actions and inactions in following the six secrets. What I did know was that this issue the dog exhibited was in him long before I came along and no one else had pushed that dog to see what he would do. Instead, they were keeping him at bay with cookies and treats and trying to get on his good side. As I observed the human relationship, I could sense that there were underlying unresolved issues there between M and his wife that no one was pushing to come clear on either.

This incident taught me to listen very clearly to what I am saying inside my head and to say what I mean, even if it feels like I might insult someone or incur his or her judgment. Now I listen to what my insides are sharing with me; I respect my inner knowing; and say what I mean and mean what I say. This gave me a lesson I will never forget.

When you ask for something of your dog, do not allow your dog to violate what you asked for or this bad behavior will continue to happen. If you are in any kind of relationship, be clear about what you are asking for: say what you mean, mean what you say, honor your word, trust and respect yourself, and claim your authentic power.

When you love, trust, and respect yourself and your dog by saying what you mean and meaning what you say, other people will respect you too.

"If a dog will not come to you after having looked you in the face, you should go home and examine your conscience."
Woodrow Wilson

Secret # 3:

Healthy Boundaries

Healthy and clear boundaries are essential to any pack. Dogs who overstep their bounds are corrected quickly within the pack. I have observed more and more dogs getting into fights because more and more dogs have unhealthy or unclear boundaries at home. This leads to the dogs being energetically out of balance, either over or under the normal balanced energy range. When a dog who is out of balance enters a situation with a dog who is balanced, the balanced dog will do the job that the humans have not done and correct that imbalance. To us, this looks like a fight, but to our dogs this looks like the natural thing to do.

If the dog being corrected is really out of balance, he/she will generally perpetuate the situation into a fight. If the dog being corrected is mildly out of balance, he/she will respect the correction and back off his/her energy and go about his/her business.

Healthy boundaries can alleviate all sorts of unacceptable behaviors such as: lunging, pulling, not coming when called, runaways, fear, aggression, testing, housebreaking, etc. Just about every behavior issue I come across in training stems from unhealthy boundaries. It is simple: your dog begins to know what he can get away with and he will keep testing you by crossing those boundaries until you become your dog's faithful leader and set and stick to clear boundaries.

Healthy boundaries allow a pack to function as a team where everyone knows their place, knows the rules, and abides by them. If they do not abide by them, the pack will correct this rather quickly. This is what allows the pack to function as a team. How well they respect boundaries is how well they will thrive.

Even though dogs have been domesticated for thousands of years, their basic, most primal instincts are to be part of a pack or family and to have a job. When we humans adopt a puppy we become his pack. The issue is that we don't exactly know what healthy boundaries are for a puppy and we generally do not know how to correct him in his own language.

Realizing the simple fact that if your puppy was in a pack, he would be given corrections if needed 24/7 is the first glimpse you may have into speaking your dog's language and learning to be a true leader.

Dogs Don't Judge Themselves

Have you ever noticed how much judgment we humans carry around with us or project at just about everything in our lives? We judge our bodies, celebrities, teachers, bosses, our kids, our spouses, ourselves, the politicians, big business, and on and on. It seems like most everything has a judgment attached to it. We are not good enough, deserving enough, pretty enough, thin enough, fast enough, smart enough, have enough. Enough is enough already!

A judgment is basically an opinion. A judgment is different than an awareness. A judgment is a point of view that carries an energy allowing what we are judging to become a reality. An awareness allows you to be aware of what is happening in the present moment without the point of view of judgment allowing you to see a bigger picture of what is taking place.

Dogs don't judge themselves. It doesn't matter what they are doing, who scolded them, who they scraped with, whether they are homeless, or whether they are heroes. Dogs simply are beings that are free of judgment. They attach no opinions to their experiences. They *will* react from past experiences. For example, a dog who was kicked by a tall man in a baseball hat may be leery of tall men or any man in a baseball hat. But the dog won't judge that person or hold an opinion of him; the dog will simply avoid that person as a survival instinct from a past experience.

When working with your dog to create clear boundaries, please remain in the present moment and don't judge your dog or puppy as good or bad. How many times have you heard someone correct a dog by yelling "bad dog" for perhaps making a mistake in the house or chewing up a favorite shoe? I know I did this when Barney was young. I had so much judgment of that dog I am amazed he still liked me.

Your dog or pup is simply learning to navigate his world and be himself. Your job as his leader is to anticipate as much as you can about what he might find of interest, to regulate his bathroom habits, to make sure that you are really clear about your boundaries for him, and to reinforce him with the correct alignment of your energy.

Maintain Healthy Boundaries Until the Lesson Is Learned

Since a dog's language is all about energy, it is important for you to know what a healthy boundary in a dog's language would look like. So I will provide you with an example here. Do you remember times in your life when your mother and father told you not to do something? Whatever it was that they told you not to do, that was a boundary. They gave you a parameter to not go beyond. And as a child, naturally you probably tested that boundary. And then they told you again, possibly in a louder tone, not to do that again. And on and on it may have escalated till you may have been sent to your room.

What your parents were intending to do was give you a healthy limit for you to learn how to harness your energy to keep you safe.

In a dog's world, when an older dog is setting boundaries for a younger dog (primarily a mom with her puppies) she does so to teach the younger dog how to survive. In our human world we don't have many predators, but wild dogs have them so they have to know from very early on how to respect the boundaries of the older dogs to ensure the survival of the pack.

When working with your dog or puppy, it is very important to remember that the energy of the boundary must be maintained until the lesson is learned or the dog will continue doing the same behavior. A mother dog will do this by keeping the intense energy on the pup until the pup gives a sigh to signal that he/she got the lesson. As the dog becomes more vested in that bad habit, it will be harder and harder to reinforce healthy boundaries. When you tell your puppy no, it should be no consistently. Too often we ask for one thing and then get lax on maintaining the energy to have our boundary respected. We cave in or allow our pooches off the hook, and then they are right back at the behavior that we don't want. The bigger they get, the bigger that bad behavior gets.

This lesson holds equally true with people. If we don't hold a clear boundary, the other person will generally violate it. It is up to you to say what you mean, mean what you say, and not allow that line to be crossed. I have often found that healthy boundaries assist me in staying true to myself.

Personal Story

I have a girlfriend since childhood I will call Jean. One day, Jean and I were on the phone during our four times a year catch-up. As we carried on our conversation, Jean began to tell me about another mutual girlfriend who had just ended her 20+ year on- again off-again relationship. As Jean began sharing this with me, I immediately felt a disconnection with her and the conversation as I had little interest in listening to this story yet again.

Jean sensed this and asked me if I felt like hearing any of it because she had felt my distance. At the moment, I truly did not feel like hearing the saga once again. I love Jean and our mutual friend, but I was over listening to one more recapitulation of that doomed relationship that had nothing to do with me. I told Jean that I really had no interest in hearing it. Jean got very upset and insulted, which normally would have triggered me into offering apologies and feeling guilt. This time though, as I had had a lot of practice learning healthy boundaries from the dogs, I did not flinch. I felt sorry that her feelings were hurt, but since I was asked for my honest feedback I provided it and held a clear boundary. Jean proceeded to get more and more upset and I let her without taking any of it on. She said she could no longer speak to me at that time and I said okay and we hung up.

What I have learned from the dogs about clear boundaries is that we are responsible for sharing our truth and honesty in a loving and caring way, but we are not responsible for the way anyone else reacts to that.

Healthy Boundaries Alleviate Trauma and Drama

When working with clients on correcting a behavior, the most important thing I can convey is the instituting of healthy boundaries. When we humans correct, we say something in a way that has the energy of our words going directly over the head of our dog or puppy. When parent dogs correct their puppies, they do so in a way that focuses a specific energy from their gut at the puppies. By keeping this energy focused on the puppies, they will not back off until the puppies back off their energy and let out a big sigh. Once the puppies back off this energy, then they are in a more receptive state to learn.

I explain this using the analogy of pushing back a loaded spring. If you correct your puppy by your normal means, you will basically be pushing back a loaded spring. If you correct your puppy or dog from the pack point of view, you will hold that corrective energy on your pooch and not back off until you get a sigh or release of the pent-up energy. You'll be doing yourself and your pup a great service because a dog who knows when to back off his/her energy has a sounder mind, is in balance, and can be trusted.

This definitely does not constitute dominating or threatening your dog. It does not mean intimidating him or her or making that dog scared of you either. It's like having a staring contest with your dog and whoever looks away first wins. It simply means that whoever holds the energy longer and more clearly wins. *You* need to be that winner.

Believe it or not, healthy boundaries are what actually change and transform relationships into unions of clarity, kindness, and awareness of self and others, not to mention a level of respect and honor you cultivate within yourself that develops into a true sense of confidence that comes from knowing yourself and knowing your dog.

And when you do have healthy boundaries, they are less likely to be violated. As a result, you will not call in people, places, or things that violate your boundaries to help you release your old beliefs so you can develop and strengthen healthier ones.

Becoming a Master of Boundaries

Boundaries are a touchy subject to many human parents of dogs. We have a challenge here because boundaries mean different things to humans than they do to our furry companions. We are built for nurturing and caring for those who are unable to care for themselves, and this is a great thing in the human world. It is also a great thing in the animal world because this compassion and nurturing makes people sensitive and protective over the animals who share our world. And it allows mothers to raise and nurture their young.

The only issue for the dogs arises when we go overboard on that human level of caring without healthy boundaries. The prime example I often see in unhealthy boundaries occurs with rescue and shelter dogs. Often times people feel so bad for the dog's prior situation that they nurture a lot of the dog's insecurities. As a result, the dog makes a certain level of progress and feels safer, but the dog also learns he/she can manipulate the people and does not have to fully move through or past the trauma.

In the dog world, an incident happens and due to the survival nature of the pack in the wild and the full presence they must bring to their life at all times, they don't have time to spend dwelling on or being stuck in their wounds. The pack must move on and let go of the past.

Boundaries to me represent saying what you mean and meaning what you say without any excuses or worries that someone won't like you for taking good care of yourself. Boundaries also give you an opportunity to be really clear about what works for you and what does not. When you are clear, there is far less trauma and drama created in your life, and there are far less situations of blame and hurt feelings. A newfound clarity occurs because you are taking full responsibility for all of your choices and realize that you are the master of your own life, so each choice is a reflection of you. And when you allow your dog to be responsible for his/her choices he/she is more aware, present, and smart.

My dog Indie, a 9-year-old male dachshund, is really quite a master of boundaries. He is very clear with other dogs what is okay and what is not. He has trained many puppies and out-of-balance dogs with me. Many times I will bring Indie with me on training sessions and get a very clear read on where the other dog is by observing Indie's reactions and responses to the dog or pup. Indie is one of the most consistent dogs I have ever had the pleasure of knowing.

Personal Insight

I am always amazed at how well Indie reads the energy levels of other dogs. During 2007 to 2009 we lived in Santa Barbara, California. It did not take us long to discover the local dog beach. There were dogs everywhere, of all sizes, breeds, ages, and temperaments.

Indie is an 18-pound dynamo. I noticed a lot of the larger dogs felt that it was okay for them to just charge him and get in his face. When the other dog was a puppy (even a large one), Indie knew he could use his energy and bark off the other dog. When it was an imbalanced older dog with an over-the-top energy, he would wait to draw the other dog in and, as soon as the dog lowered his energy, Indie made sure to let him know who was in charge. What's astonishing to me was that in every situation he knew how to read those dogs to a "T".

In watching Indie with the pups I have raised in my own home, it was so clear to me that it is not the size of the dog in the fight, it's the size of the fight in the dog. Not that he would fight with my pups, he just set clear unwavering boundaries. Even as they grew and towered over him, all Indie had to do was lift his lip and my pups backed off immediately. They still do to this day, even though they outweigh him by well over 45 pounds.

I learned a long time ago that a dog can correct another dog better than I will ever be able to. So I find it helpful to have Indie along because of the confidence, independence, and balance he maintains. Not only will he correct another dog without hesitation, and do so honorably, but he'll also show the other dog what it is to be a balanced being. I need to put that dog on my payroll!

Boundaries are necessary to create a properly socialized, well-balanced mind in any dog. This is the case not only with a challenged dog who may be lunging, or a submissive dog who is having a hard time being confident, but also with the over-exuberant, super-playful dog. A dog with this personality may be over-the-brink energetically for most other dogs and can usually be found pulling his/her owner down the street.

As I work with more dogs and people, it becomes clearer to me that where the person is allowing the dog to break his/her boundaries is where the person's boundaries are not clearly defined and healthy. I cannot tell you the amount of times I have seen people's entire lives change as a result of learning to have clearer boundaries with their dogs.

Will This Boundary Stuff Work with My Kids?

Human parents often ask me if this boundary stuff will work with their kids. They've witnessed how effective clearing up their boundaries with their dogs has worked. I always smile and say, "Yes it does."

Please note I am not comparing dogs to children. I am saying that un-channeled, bounding energy displayed by both children and puppies needs to be harnessed and channeled in proper ways so that it can develop and grow in a balanced and healthy system.

One of the best continuous examples I can give you of this is when parents get clear and unemotionally attached with giving their dogs healthy boundaries on what is okay and what is not. Then they start employing the same clarity with their children. I have literally watched dozens of family structures change and old "guilt" patterns fade away as a result of working with their dogs.

In all cases of dog behavior, I take my cues of proper and healthy boundaries from the dogs themselves. I am constantly observing what dogs do to keep themselves and the other dogs around them in balance.

Personal Insight

My puppy, Aiyana, is showing me amazing things about how boundaries can be playful and flexible but also extremely clear. From the time I brought her home at ten weeks old, she would allow Indie to correct her, but also stand up for herself if he went overboard. I was amazed as I watched her at the dog park. She loves to play with her friend Izzy, a husky puppy about seven weeks younger. The girls are a blast to watch as they vie back and forth to see who is top dog; they will go at it for an hour without a break. They tolerate a lot from one another, but should another dog that Yana senses is trying to dominate them come over, she will stand nose to nose with that dog or back up and give a warning snap that the other dog needs to back up.

I knew within two months of bringing her home that Yana would be a lead female. I observed how she handled herself with a large male German shepherd, who must have weighed more than 100 pounds and was interested in following her around while she played with Izzy. He began trying to herd her and separate the two girls. At first Yana tried to get away from him, but when he persisted in wanting to mount her, she swung around, stared him straight in the eye, and as he got in closer to her face, she snapped at him. He backed off instantly.

I am enjoying this new learning curve as I realize the responsibility I have to help shape Yana's Authentic Leadership personality in the most beautiful of ways. Setting clear boundaries with her, being playful, yet clear about when something is a no, learning to be a great leader to her, and tending her needs for exercise, companionship, and downtime has brought a new level of clarity and inner calm to my own life.

Boundaries and Anger: Instilling Trust or Fear

Boundaries and anger are two very different energies. The potency of each can leave positive or negative energy imprints that either instill trust or fear in your dog or pup.

When a mother dog corrects, she corrects to instantly cut the behavior the dog is exhibiting. If you have ever witnessed this taking place, it can be very harsh and loud, spurring the puppy to scream. Mom means business. In the wild she has to teach her pups to survive on his/her own. She is not interested in her pup's opinion about things; she is only interested in teaching him/her to survive and in her own survival. So when she corrects, she is doing so from a place of totally clear boundaries. In human terms it would be like someone drawing a line in the sand and saying, "Don't cross it."

The energy of healthy boundaries comes from someone totally in control of his or her emotions who is aware of his/her inner power. This person knows that just by a look he or she can convey his/her strength without having to have it go any further. Healthy boundaries infer that a conflict need never escalate as the person is comfortable with himself or herself and knows his/her yes's and no's. This person needs only raise energy enough for someone to realize that he or she is beginning to cross a line.

Anger, on the other hand, is generally not coming from a place of healthy boundaries. Anger is coming from a place of ego where you take it as a personal affront that the pup or dog has done something to you. Now you start feeling some other old unhealed emotion that generally has nothing to do with the current situation that has triggered you beyond your control.

From my experience in situations involving dogs or humans, anger always loses. Let me clarify here that I am talking about the type of anger that exacts reaction, revenge, resentment, or rage. These are all examples of out-of-control anger, and if you try to work with your dog or puppy from this place you will not be such an effective leader.

I wish to distinguish this type of anger from anger as a potent energy that motivates one to take the necessary action to have clear boundaries. This is often the case with really timid dogs who are in fear. Once the fear gets past a certain point it will turn to the energy of anger, at which point the dog will usually snap. When the dog snaps, he or she is generally protecting himself/herself but needs that anger to be able to do so. In the wild, most animals function from anger as a potent energy needed to eat and survive. It is not personal and it does not last longer than the situation.

If you are looking to work with your puppy or dog in the most beneficial way possible, I suggest you begin by observing yourself and noticing if your boundaries with your dog are healthy and clear or muddled with unresolved anger.

I learned this difference a long time ago with my chocolate lab. One day I saw myself so frustrated, angry, and out of control when correcting him for not coming to me that I literally sat and cried because I realized I was taking my unresolved pain of not knowing how to get what I need out on him. It was a huge breakthrough for me as I had never before realized I was doing to him what had been done to me. I was unconsciously operating out of the pattern I had witnessed my parents exhibit whenever I did not listen to them as a child. Then they sent anger, frustration, and rage in my direction, as they took it very personally when I did not do what they wanted me to. Clearly I needed to change that old pattern. I thank my lab so much because that day changed my life forever.

When you come from a place of anger or taking something personally, you will lose.

Not much in life is a personal affront, only another thing to move through and enjoy eventually.

Use your anger as a potency to transform a challenging situation into something that works for all, not as a weapon to hurt another. I see this happen so often in human relationships between parents and children. The child is acting out in need of something he or she usually cannot describe, and the parent takes it as a personal affront and corrects out of anger. Few parents I observe these days have or set healthy boundaries with their kids. Perhaps that is why they ask me after they start training and setting boundaries with the pups whether this approach would work with their kids or husband.

We all need boundaries, healthy ones but boundaries nevertheless. This is not to imply a boundary as a limitation; it's to say that boundaries make us feel safer and assist us in channeling our energy more effectively. It's like the puppy who is just so out of control you kind of secretly hope he or she gets walloped by another dog. It's also like the kid screaming in the restaurant while the parents do nothing; you hope the manager asks them to leave. The puppy and kid are both craving a healthy boundary so they can feel that they can stop escalating their energy and relax. Often it is done to get attention that they need but don't know how to request.

I can virtually guarantee you that once you start becoming very comfortable with healthy boundaries with your dog or pup, you will see a noticeable decrease in any trauma and drama you may be experiencing. I can also virtually guarantee that you will see an increase in pleasurable moments of deepened connection and communication with your dog as you relax into your Authentic Leadership and they relax into their natural follower position.

"I would look at a dog and when our eyes met, I realized that the dog and all creatures are my family. They're like you and me."
Ziggy Marley

Secret # 4:
Creating the Energy Connection

Love Your Dog in His/Her Own Language

Everything that exists on this planet—from the smallest to largest creatures, air, water, earth, blades of grass, molecules—is connected by invisible threads of energy that share the same essence at their core. Beyond or underneath the physical there is an unseen connection that can only be experienced when we become quiet and motionless and feel the invisible threads of energy that connect us all.

Dogs are connected to this invisible energy field all of the time. Their silence is to their advantage in staying connected to this field. Our words are to our disadvantage, even though we are aware that this field exists. Dogs are born into a world of silence where they learn to develop their skills of hearing, sensing, seeing, tasting, touching, and smelling in a very pure way. There are very few contortions in the way they understand their world through this energy because most of it is not filled with emotional baggage; instead it is simple, pure, and accurate.

Human love has many facets. Often times those facets involve unhealed emotional wounds from the past that get mixed in with our love even for our dogs. We apply human love to our dogs. In many ways this is confusing to them because we tend to have an emotional neediness in our love that dogs do not have in their world. In our human world, we give love with the expectation of getting it back. Our love has conditions and often times baggage. Sometimes we will do things to ensure that our love is reciprocated so we can feel validated; if our love is not reciprocated then we're emotionally shunned and we tend to feel insulted which could lead to us shutting down or holding back.

In your dog's world, love is based on a silent communication of respect. Voices need never be raised because respect is a silent expression, which dogs often convey with the look of their eyes or the hair on the back of their necks standing up to communicate various levels of intensity or dominance. When dogs demonstrate love to each other, it's coming from a place of respect, not from a place of needing to validate who and what they are about. For them it is simple: Am I accepted as a part of the pack and where do I fit in?

When we humans take a puppy into our home and love him or her in our human way, we tend to allow that pup to break tons of boundaries every single minute that he or she is in our house. Our human love tends to have far less clear-cut boundaries because we are having fun watching our pup explore his or her world from a human heart/emotional place. We are not teaching that pup survival mode like the mother dog would because in our care he/she has less survival issues to worry about than in the wild. This can lead to really big problems. Remember, if that puppy was with his or her mother, she would be training that puppy 24/7 every single day. That mother dog's job is to make sure that her puppy stays alive. In order to accomplish that, when the mother dog sees that her puppy is exhibiting certain behaviors, she's going to tell that puppy in no uncertain terms that that behavior is absolutely not acceptable. The unacceptable behavior could mean the difference between life and death for that puppy.

A correction can occur when the pup gets too far outside of Mom's energy comfort zone, when the pup is playing too rough with another pup, or when the pup is going to eat something that Mom senses is harmful.

When we bring puppies home, or in the case of a rescue dog who we discover was abused and treated poorly and/or starved, what we immediately do is apply our human love. We want the dog to feel better. We do everything we can as we try to serve the dog by making him feel better or comfort him like we would a child. Straightaway, the dog figures out, "Hmm, I can actually manipulate this situation."

So instead of starting out as very clear leaders to our new dog, providing the proper food, exercises, and healthy boundaries, we actually feed into the dog's insecurity because we want to make our new dog better because we will feel successful if our dog feels better and happy. In addition, we also tend to give love to get the dog to return our love. This situation is not so great if we want to help our dog rebalance his/her emotional states relatively quickly or help raise our new puppy in the clearest manner possible.

One of the things that I recommend to my clients, especially for a new puppy or for a rescue dog, is to begin to learn to love the dog in his/her own language. Dogs in the wild are rarely psychologically screwed up or neurotic because the pack has to function and each dog has to know his/her place and purpose. When a puppy or rescue dog comes to us, we pretty much give that dog free reign and then, when that dog starts acting out or behaving in ways we don't like, we start shortening up the leash (no pun intended).

The problem with this is that we've allowed the dog to start establishing certain habits that probably aren't so favorable to the dog or us. Let's take the case of an abused dog who entered a dog pack. That dog pack is actually going to pick on that dog till he/she lets go of old experiences and actually becomes a functional member of that pack. Otherwise, in all likelihood, the pack would kill that dog.

When we try to love a new puppy from a human perspective, and we don't provide proper and healthy boundaries, we're setting that dog up for failure because he/she doesn't know what his/her place should be in the pack or what his/her job is. And in our modern-day world, we've created dogs as strictly pets so they don't have to have a job to do as in the past. Their only job is basically learning what we need them to do and how we need them to be in our lives, which is an essential part of training.

Loving our animals in their language means making sure that boundaries are very, very clear. No really means no. When you ask your dog to come over here, it means come over here right now. When you tell your dog to leave something he or she must leave it immediately. Training then becomes a consistent routine instead of becoming something that you do one hour every day; training becomes something that you do every single time you're with that puppy or that dog. It becomes incorporated into your life naturally. Dogs love consistency and a leader they can count on to be clear and consistent.

"It's no coincidence that man's best friend cannot talk." -Anonymous

Silent Energy is Much More Powerful than Words

Dogs don't communicate with all the different words that we humans use to communicate with each other. Dogs communicate silently through telepathic pictures, vocalizations, and body language.

For instance, a dog bowing down on his front legs with his tail in the air is signaling "I want to play with you." Flattening of the ears, with the tail straight back and the hackles up signals dominance: "I am going to check you out and if you resist or react, I may attack you." A big grin with the tongue hanging out signals a happy dog. A tail tucked under the butt signals fear, often along with nervousness and anxiety and uncertainty. A dog lying on his side and getting lower than another dog or urinating in the other dog's presence signals submission.

It's always fascinating to watch dogs as they play and make their way around the park because they will figure out very quickly who they like, who they don't want to be around, who's safe, who's going to start a fight, who they can get a ball from—and it's all basically done silently.

We humans use so many words to convey and explain what we want. Most of the time it's pretty humorous that we don't actually get what we want even though we have all these words to describe our desires. One of the reasons why I created the Walk In Sync™ System was because it helps us communicate with our dogs in their language of energy which is silence. This system emits a powerful energy by allowing you to grip the leash to provide a consistent amount of room to your dog and by allowing you to cue your dog's body through the specially fitted harness. So instead of saying things and repeating them a bunch of times, we actually say less, get clearer pictures in our minds, and get more from our dogs because we're starting to communicate with them in *their* language.

As a trainer, I've always found it interesting the amount of words we use as we try to teach our dogs what we want when our dog's strongest form of communication is not verbal but rather visual. So we have been using words rather than perfecting pictures to get what we want from our dogs and then using our words to back it up. We're actually doing all of this backwards. Communicating in our dog's language means becoming quiet enough to tune into our dog's bodies, what they're aware of, and what they're focusing on. In that silence, we can command the space to have our dogs return their focus to us as their leaders. But in order for dogs to focus on us, we have to become more silent and embody the energy of being a true leader in order to transform into their leaders.

> # "Lots of people talk to animals.... Not very many listen, though.... That's the problem."
> ## -Benjamin Hoff, *The Tao of Pooh*

Learning Nature's Language: Telepathic Connection and Communication

I have loved dogs and other animals my entire life. I've spent my life around an assortment of animals: dogs, cats, rabbits, horses, and turtles. I can't really remember a time in my life (except for two years after my divorce) that I didn't have my dogs on a full-time basis. They've really made a huge difference in my life.

At age 24 I began studying Qigong—a form of internal martial arts—with a Chinese energy master. Qigong is a series of simple movements that helps the body attune back to its natural state of balance, bringing it back into harmony and connection with nature. As I continued my Qigong studies, I uncovered my ability to hear the plants and the animals and other messages from nature, which I had been closed off from. Qigong actually helped me re-attune to the information and messages that were around me all the time in the natural world that I hadn't able to hear anymore.

As a result of my Qigong practice, I ventured to a workshop in Hawaii to study with an animal communicator. During the workshop we did an exercise that allowed us to uncover "the belief behind the belief behind the belief" about anything. One of the questions that the facilitator had asked was, "What was your first belief about animals?" As we sat and meditated, all of the participants had different beliefs come up. As they came up, the facilitator would ask us, "Well what is the belief behind that? And who did it belong to?"

I found this to be one of the primary exercise I have incorporated into assisting humans in getting to the root of any belief so I would love to share it with you now. It is a really powerful exercise to be able to see if our beliefs are truly our own or if we picked them up from someone else. If the latter, we can now let them go to discover our own truth. Please feel free to take the next five or so minutes to do the exercise below.

Exercise:

Sit in a comfortable chair that embraces you and allows you to relax. Start by closing your eyes (after you read this) and breathing into your nose. Fill up your belly with air and exhale through your nose, allowing your belly to gently press against your lower back. Repeat five to ten times. As your body relaxes from receiving more oxygen, allow your eyes to begin looking inward as you drop more deeply into your body.

Ask yourself the question," What was my first belief or memory about animals in my life?" Continue breathing in a relaxed manner and allow yourself to notice what memories are revealed.

Was it yours or someone else's belief? Ask who does that belief belong to. And once you know it's not yours, simply ask yourself what is it that is your truest belief about animals that you gave up and replaced with someone else's awareness?

What did you learn about whose beliefs you were actually carrying around? And about what your true beliefs are?

If you would like more information on how to learn to telepathically communicate with your animals, please see product information at the back of this book to purchase my Animal Communication Home Study Course.

What I came to see from that exercise was that my very first belief/memory was that "animals are untrustworthy and therefore not safe and that they are inferior to humans." I came to realize that this belief was not even my own; it belonged to the adults around me who believed that they were protecting me by making me very cautious of animals. I learned that I knew all along that I could talk with the animals and that we could communicate in a language that was beyond human words. I always knew that the animal kingdom held more of a vibration of home, safety, and comfort to me than the human world.

After that process I was able to lift a lot of layers and a lot of veils that I had used to cover up what my actual true beliefs were about the animal kingdom and my innate ability to connect with animals and communicate with them.

For those of you unfamiliar with telepathic communication, I will make it as simple as I am able. Telepathy is the ability to communicate with one another using no verbal or spoken words. It is an ability that every life form on the planet possesses. Think of telepathy as the universal language. Since telepathy involves communicating in pictures (which are a universal language of communication) you don't need to speak the same verbal language, you just share pictures with one another and each being in the conversation understands the other even if the verbal languages differ. I call this the language of the heart because it's universal.

As a result of that workshop where I experienced my first communication with dolphins, I became a professional animal communicator. As the natural or alternative healing arts fascinated me, I started an Animal Wellness Consulting practice. There I began applying different types of energy healing work to animals and communicating with the animals on a telepathic level. I listened to what the animals had to say in order to assist their humans in finding out what was wrong with their ill animals and how to help them heal. I would also ask my animal clients about their perspectives: what they thought of their lives, of their situations, and of certain behaviors that they were exhibiting.

It was during this time of doing my communication work that I started training dogs. I began utilizing the technique of telepathy, visualizing a specific picture of what I wanted while asking the dog for what I wanted. I also had my clients visualize with their dogs. I would ask them to have the dog sit, and most of the time the dogs weren't sitting. Then I would ask them to picture in their mind what the dog looked like when he/she sat down and then again ask the dog to sit. About 98 percent of the time, when my clients started getting really clear with their pictures, their dogs responded so much more quickly because the level of communication had become so much clearer.

It would be wise for us to understand that our dogs' primary form of communication is pictures. Humans have been trying to teach our dogs solely through words, and the one main component that we've been missing is adding pictures to our dialogue.

When we are working with our dogs and creating a deeper energy connection, it's imperative that we connect with these animals from their first language, which is pictures. All humans are born with telepathy, but it's been conditioned out of us and most of us don't use it anymore. So it's really incredibly helpful not only in working with our dogs but also in reconnecting with the natural world. Once we regain that silent inner knowing and intuition, we'll achieve a whole new sense of clarity by being clear about the pictures we're placing in our minds and what we're actually requesting of our dogs.

It's been said that our thoughts create our world. Then it would be imperative that we actually pay attention to what our thoughts are. It is important for our thoughts to be in alignment with our words and our intentions. That is where animals always reside. That's why their world is a lot clearer than ours.

Intimacy Lessons: Being in Tune with You and Your World

One of the most important things I have learned from my dogs and all of the dogs I have worked with is the power of being tuned in with myself and the world around me. It is this presence that has saved me many times from being injured by animals I am working with or working on. The silence allowed me to sense a horse turning quickly with his mouth open so I could pull my hand away before being bit or a dog ready to launch at an unsuspecting child.

This being in tune with oneself and one's world is the place where dogs live. Their hearing frequency is about 40 Hz to 60,000 Hz compared to the human hearing frequency of 20 Hz to 20,000 Hz. Dogs have 220 million olfactory receptors in their noses, while humans have only 5 million. Dogs' sight is more sensitive than humans as they are able to see things more clearly in dim light and at longer ranges and to detect subtle movements more accurately. And the biggest difference: dogs took a vow of silence. When you are silent all of your senses are more active and alert. This silence is what allows them to stay tuned into the world around them because they can only deal with what is in the moment. Humans can make up many different versions of what is happening and create really interesting stories around it, which often keeps us from the truth.

We humans have developed a four-second attention span. From our newscasts to our conversations to our texts to interacting with our children to choosing our foods, we have become an extremely fast-paced society who is disconnected from our essence—the core of who we really are. And we're disconnected from the truth of what we really require in each moment. Remember, children are not born with ADD, they learn it. They learn it from us adults who think we are so together but are so disconnected from our own sense of self that that is exactly what we pass along to our children and our dogs.

Dogs have never lost this connection of being tuned into their core. Unbalanced dogs, those with neurotic problems, and those with psychological problems because of poor conditioning and training have all lost this sense of being tuned in. However, these are more human-based issues rather than animal-based issues.

Dogs don't have a million thoughts running through their minds. They're not racing around trying to figure out how to work and get the kids to soccer and who's cooking dinner. It's a much simpler world. Dogs go out in an open way. They stay clear, play, and have fun. They keep life really, really simple. And it's very easy for them to be intimate with each other because they're connected to their core.

One of the things that I have found is that dogs assist me in coming back to that quiet, centered space within myself. This is the place where I am most intimate with myself. When we get quiet and we show up in the present moment for our dogs, that's all that's really required for reconnecting with the intimacy of who we are, where we are in the moment, and what we're asking for. It's a very simple yet valuable process that dogs bring us back to.

Intimacy is something we have disconnected ourselves from in modern society. I watch the animals and how they are able to navigate and move through things so quickly. Then I contrast this intimacy with the relationships between friends, spouses, parents, and children. In these relationships I observe that there is a lack of intimacy; it's consistently being eroded because we're not connected to ourselves anymore. We're not connected to how we truly feel; instead we're more connected to what we want or what we think rather than who we actually are.

In spending time and quiet moments with dogs, I observe them when they're at rest and at play, and watch how beautifully they can navigate between rest and play. It's in those quiet, silent moments spent with my dogs or with the dogs I'm training that everything else falls away. The thoughts of the day, the shopping and to-do lists, bad feelings, guilty feelings, challenging feelings all vanish. When we actually allow ourselves to connect into the center of who we are and reconnect with our intimacy, we are filled with so much beautiful light, and at the same time filled with so much darkness and challenge.

When we drop into the center and become fully present, there is a certain level of balance that comes back to us. I see it in the dogs who are really balanced and happy and playful, those who can also raise their tails in alarm at one moment and then the next moment wag their tails with happiness. It's amazing to watch them navigate and how quickly they steer through those states because they're connected with themselves and stay in the present moment. And it's been a beautiful process to watch when working with a person and dog team. It's not just about training the dog on habits and behaviors. It is rewarding to watch a totally type A personality reconnect with the intimacy and the quietness and the stillness that this person channels to be fully present for his/her dog.

I really do believe that this is one of the greatest gifts dogs came here to share with us: how to reconnect with that intimacy of the truth of who we are and to allow ourselves to be fully present. Dogs are not afraid to come over to us and stick their heads under our arms and ask for a pat, or wag their tails and say, "Hey, it's time for a break so let's go out now!" And it is in these levels of intimacy that dogs are so humongously helpful in reminding us how to be more humane to ourselves and how to reconnect with the intimacy and the truth of who we really are. They show us on the deepest levels how to be in tune with ourselves, which in turn helps us to be in tune with the world. And it is that energy connection I find to be one of the greatest gifts that dogs can teach us.

Dogs Understand Love as a Trustworthy Leader Who Takes Care of the Pack

When you are training your dog and teaching a new command that your dog is picking up pretty quickly on his way to mastery, there is a natural euphoria you experience as you build the relationship and the skills. Then once you go outside, it's as if your devoted dog who was just doing so well has no clue who you are or why you are running after him in a panic with your arms flailing wildly as your dog continues to run away.

Has this ever happened to you? Did you project an air of anger, frustration, and resentment at your dog for making you feel scared that he could get hurt? It has happened to me more times in my life than I would care to count. And I did exactly what I am going to advise you not do: "I took every single incident personally."

When I was raising my dog Tucson, I really believed that once I trained him a couple of times he would become perfect. When he did not, I cannot even describe the level of insult and personal offense I took with that. I had no clue what dogs thought, knew, believed, cared about, or understood back then. All I knew was that I was the master and he was the dog. Let's just say, my ex-boyfriend was a far better trainer to him than I was. And because my ex understood energy far more than I did at the time, he and Tucson had really clear boundaries and a great relationship. What my ex knew was that he was in charge; what Toose knew was that he had a great leader he could follow and he did not take anything personally. Toose and I adored each other but it would not be until later that I would come to understand how to best work with a dog from an energy perspective and not take anything personally.

It was not until I got Barney that I really became aware that when you come from a place of anger or take something personally you will lose. Not much in life is a personal affront, only another thing to move through and enjoy. And that's what dogs do: they experience something and move through it as joyfully as they can and then move onto the next experience as fully as they can. Authentic Leaders don't take things personally; they allow for others' opinions and keep to their path moving all who follow them along.

Use Your Anger as a Potency to Transform a Challenging Situation

When humans take things personally, we generally tend to react with anger or fear. What I have learned in working with dogs is that anger expressed by humans is energetically different than when animals express it. Anger in the human world is generally tied into not getting what we want, or being violated or lied to. Anger more often than not is an emotion and a personal affront in the human world. We have anger; we may suppress anger; and we may use anger as a weapon against another. We usually find some kind of reason and/or justification for holding onto our anger by keeping our story about our anger alive.

We start wars over our anger, but have you ever heard of a dog in the history of the world who started a war? If a dog has an issue, he or she will handle it right then and there, in most cases. There are definitely cases where a dog will hold onto anger and wait for revenge, but from what I have observed those dogs had a host of other behavioral issues as well.

Anger in the dog world is about clarification of boundaries and who is in charge. In a dog's world anger is a potency that the animals are choosing to be to get what they need to survive, to keep order, to establish rank, or to get what they want. A potency is a state of being the fullest expression of whatever you are feeling without regard for what anyone else thinks about it. Think of a male lion strutting around the jungle. Is there any question about him embodying his potency as the king of the jungle? This is where our animals can teach us so much about the essence of embodying our true potency, even if it is anger. They embody it fully when they need to and then let it go.

Personal Story

My dog Aiyana made a new friend, Meela. Meela is a shepherd /husky mix. Meela is a great girl but not completely sure yet about her role in a pack when Aiyana is around. She is not sure if she is top dog. Meela sometimes tries to pull rank in a little bit of a shady way that could put other dogs on guard to be aggressive. Meela is more apt to sink her head down and prepare for a fight to establish her role. This is not a bad thing, but Meela's guardian and I keep a watch out for the slightest signal of hair raising on her back when she and Aiyana meet because we want to stop that type of energy flow at the very beginning before anything escalates.

Aiyana is pretty confident of her role. She knows she can take care of herself in pretty much any situation and she will greet other dogs immediately with clarity and then take them under her wing.

The other day the girls were playing in the snow and something must have set one of them off and they started scraping with each other. I yelled for them to stop but they weren't paying any attention to me. There were no wounds and no blood; it just sounded bad. I pulled them off one another and sent each one in different directions. About three minutes later I called both girls over and let them know through my energy that this behavior was not okay. They each took a deep breath, as did I and walked off. No trauma and drama, no more scraping or sulking, just giving each other space. And in 10 minutes they were playing with one another again. When it was time for Meela to go she didn't want to.

Now, had this been two humans (like females on any of the Housewives of Beverly Hills, Miami, New Jersey, New York, or Atlanta shows), those women would still be in a huff, playing into the trauma and drama of the situation, plotting their revenge, keeping up their story, and trying to get others to side with them. This is the difference between emotional anger and the potency of anger. The potency of anger allows you to express anger in an honest, authentic manner in the moment and be done with it; whereas when you're just being angry you tend to hold onto it and it will lead to more fights somewhere down the road.

I recently learned about how to see anger from a different perspective. Anger is generally seen as an unleashing of negative or pent-up emotions on someone who may or may not deserve it. In my experience with humans for the most part, anger is never really about the current situation. Anger is generally a place we go to when we are experiencing a trigger or charge from a past situation that we are carrying into the present one. Anger is also generally the secondary emotion, the primary one being hurt, fear, or sadness. Most of us would rather not feel those so we choose anger as the prime emotion because that will allow us to distance ourselves from the real truth of what we are feeling. So anger is generally a secondary emotion in human terms. It's interesting to note that most people use the energy of anger to stop something from happening, to right a wrong, or to protect themselves from their true feelings.

Our dogs are far better masters of embodying the potency of anger because when they feel, they just act out on it to clear up the current situation and move on. In a dog's world the size of the potency generally wins. So it's like I mentioned about Indie before: it's not the size of the dog in the fight but the size of the fight in the dog. For a little dog of 18 pounds, I have watched him use his potency to back off 100 plus pounds of dogs who then gave him total respect of space.

When we allow ourselves to judge our anger as a "bad thing," this then leads us to suppress it (and we all know how that usually goes). When we allow ourselves to express anger in a healthy, clear manner, a lot can transform in the relationship. Once the potency transforms the energy, then it's time to PLAY!

Play Time Is Essential to Your Dog's Well-Being…and Your Own

I don't know about you but one of the highlights of any day includes watching my dogs play. The way they run around, play tag, wrestle, greet other dogs, the sheer joy of watching my Aiyana run through fields at full speed, or my Indie dachshund trotting with his ears flapping in the wind, or Cleopatra my basset hound picking up speed to catch up just puts the biggest smile on my face and in my heart. There is something inside of me that remembers freedom and fun each time I watch my dogs play.

How many times have you been typing away at your computer or in a funk and your dog just comes over and drops a ball or a toy at your feet as if to say, "It's okay human, you need to take a break now. Come and play with me and you will feel better."

The truth is that much of what makes up a dog's life is contained in play. It's actually a four-letter word that you want to use a lot. Dogs learn through playing. Think about a litter of pups. They are always playing, testing boundaries, wrestling, or grabbing at some body part in order to inspire play in the other dog. Play builds a sensitivity to touch, clear boundaries, improves communication, and builds muscles from lots of different angles.

Play is as essential to our dog's health as proper nutrition and water.

When do we tend to lose that sense of play in our lives? Once we get into school and have to take tests and then learn to judge ourselves according to a score? Or when we feel the pressure to wear the proper clothes or suffer being made fun of? Or when we go to college to get a "serious" career? Or after we get married and have kids?

Does your dog ever really choose to no longer play? And if he/she does, what could be going on with him/her? Could a rib be out of place, perhaps hips are sore and need a chiropractic adjustment or an acupuncture session or some herbs to help him/her maintain health? Perhaps his/her nutrition needs some adjustments.

Play is a natural state for dogs and humans alike. It seems that it's only when we become too grown up, too mature that we lose that sense. Your dog is an amazing playmate, so make sure to honor that sense of play every day. It keeps you and your dog young at heart and ready for a new adventure.

Insider Tip: Learn to Shake It Off

Aside from shaking off after getting wet, have you ever noticed how your dog after experiencing a stressful experience will just "shake it off"? I have observed this phenomena quite often with dogs and their humans struggling with the clarity of who is in charge. Once the dog is released from the leash after a "battle of wills" walk, the dog will immediately either shake himself off or go to the carpet or his bed and roll around in familiar energy.

When a dog has a stressful experience he tends to clear his own energy field by shaking off the previous experience and getting more fully back into the present ness of the now. I have done this often after a stressful encounter with someone or a stressful experience. It works wonders because when I shake out my entire body and spine, the energy of the incident does not have time to take root in my spine. Furthermore, I'll refrain from making up an entire story about the encounter, which I would then lock into the memory of my central nervous system where I would continue perpetuating the story and re-experiencing the shock or stimulation of it as well.

"I think we are drawn to dogs because they are the uninhibited creatures we might be if we weren't certain we knew better."
George Bird Evans

Secret # 5:

Be an Authentic Leader

Stop Checking in with Your Dog

One of the biggest things that I began to notice when my clients start using the Walk In Sync™ System is how much people are checking in with their dogs. Your dog knows one of two things: either you're in charge or your dog is in charge. That's simply part of pack mentality. Someone has to be the leader and someone has to be the follower. I was amazed how many times I would see people start walking their dogs and instead of looking straight ahead of them they start looking to the right or to the left, whichever side the dog happens to be on. They're constantly asking the dog the question, "So where do you want to go?" Then they're shocked because the dog is leading the walk. Every time you turn and look to your dog for a direction, your dog is going to take the lead and start walking in front of you because your dog is going to assume that you've given him/her the leadership position.

One of the things that I recommend off the bat when you start walking your dog is to not keep looking down at or checking in with your dog. A leader is not going to check in with his follower every three minutes. A leader is going to lead. I often ask my clients, "If you keep looking to your right, doesn't that increase the possibility of walking into a tree?" So they quickly get the message that a walk is not designed to check in with the dog. The walk is designed for the human to be the leader and for the dog to follow the person's leadership. Eventually this will work into a partnership with both human and dog embodying balanced energy. But in order to do so you need to become a confident and relaxed leader.

One of the reasons why I put handles and grips on the leash was so that when you are walking you know exactly how much room your dog has. Remember Secret #1: consistency. You've got 24 inches from your hand to where the leash clips onto the dog's harness. And when your dog pulls to the end of the leash, you need to stop, stand still, and relax. Do not start checking in with your dog. Remain the clear leader and allow your dog to take responsibility for the fact that he or she is now putting too much pressure on the leash. Your dog will make the choice to back off of pressure. Our dogs are very smart and capable of thinking. And most of our training methods have taught our dogs not necessarily to think but to react. We want to create happy, healthy, thinking dogs who understand that when they apply pressure they can also make the choice to back off. When your dog actually chooses to back off of pressure before you correct him or her, then you have a dog who's actually walking in sync with his or her leader: you. When the dog chooses to back off pressure, he or she has made a choice that will now change his/her brainwaves; when you make the choice, it simply interrupts the dog's behavior but the dog has not made a new choice and will continue doing whatever he or she was doing until the next correction.

I'm Okay, You're Okay Syndrome

One of the main things that I have seen happen over the last decade as a professional trainer is that every time you check in with your dog, you are consistently feeding your dog's energy. This is giving your dog the power to be the leader, and you're giving away your power as leader. I'll watch somebody walk away with his/her dog and they're both looking back and forth at each other not knowing who's in charge because they're both thinking, "I'm okay, you okay?" This is not the most beneficial way to work with your dog.

You as a leader need the confidence to say, "Okay, let's go and we're going in this direction," and then lead your dog in that direction. If you do this consistently, your dog is going to start building trust in you as a leader because you are clear about the direction you are moving in, you protect and keep him/her safe, and it's a fun experience. Dogs naturally want to follow you. They willingly want to work with you.

Remember one thing: dogs were designed to work. Even though they're here as man's (and woman's) best friend, they were originally bred to do jobs. And the dogs of today are really pretty jobless. Their only real jobs are to go with us to the park, go outside and go potty, fetch a ball if we throw it, and just basically be our companions. So from the dog's point of view we haven't really allowed him or her to exercise his/her fullest potential.
Using the Walk In Sync™ System brings back a little bit more accountability to our dogs so they start thinking about where their feet are and what they're doing. This system gives them more of an awareness that they are working for us and with us, as opposed to dogs on flexi leads who are leading the walk. These dogs don't really have a purpose; they're just going out and doing their thing, but they don't really have an aim of adhering or pleasing their human leaders. And in my opinion, I have seen how that that lack of purpose, that lack of direction of a clear leader, and the lack of clear boundaries has deeply affected our dogs the most in terms of training. When a dog is leading the walk, he or she is now responsible to be the leader, which means that dog's responsible for the pack, including you.

If you have a dog who is not necessarily a leader and is not calm, relaxed, and clear about his/her job and position leading the walk, then you've created stress, over stimulation, anxiety, and nervousness in a dog who wasn't designed to lead the walk. It may look like your dog is happy clawing his/her way down the street and trying to run to the park and get there before anybody else, but he or she is not actually calm and relaxed. Your dog's energy state is actually raised, and it's when your dog is in that state that fights break out. That's where behaviors that are not desirable stem from because the dog is already in the heightened state of awareness now that he or she is leading the walk and has got to protect you. So it makes the dog actually anxious. My goal with Walk In Sync™ is to end the "I'm okay, you're okay" syndrome and have the human become the dog's leader in a very safe, effective, simple way. This will ultimately rebalance the relationship quickly with as much clarity for human and dog as possible.

Give an Inch, They'll Take A Mile

When I begin working with puppies, I highly discourage using flexi leads. When your puppy is on this type of lead, he or she learns that as soon as he/she hits a boundary the human will give the puppy more room to actually go farther away and lead the walk. I find I get the best results for my clients and myself by setting a specific amount of length that your puppy gets on the leash, which creates a very clear boundary for how far your puppy can roam. This will help you ensure and solidify the energetic connection that you have with your puppy, eventually making it much easier for off-leash training. However, if you give the puppy too much room before he or she is ready, you can be creating the problem of the dog deciding to pull rank and choosing to be dominant.

Remember, mother dogs give their pups a specific amount of room to roam before they go and get them. This amount is always small in the beginning and expands as the pups grow. This is because it is far easier for Mom to correct an undesirable behavior when the pups are closer and small, as opposed to when the behavior is much larger as is the pup.

When working with pups, I recommend using a six-foot leash. I designed our Accu-Grip™ Leash so that you start out using a six-foot leash with a short distance handle and then eventually move to the next handle distance. This will make it very clear when your puppy hits that boundary and starts pulling. Then you should stop and wait for the dog to back up his/her energy. The dog learns very quickly how to adhere to the boundaries and makes the choice to back off his/her pressure.

So I am actually an advocate of not giving them so much room right from the beginning. Give them less room and then they can earn it because that's what happens in the dog world. They actually earn more freedom, and this is what we want. We want and need our dogs to be working. They were designed with very intelligent minds and unfortunately we haven't been shaping that intelligence enough. It's time to allow our dogs to become more aware of their bodies in space and time. It's time for us to become better leaders to our dogs by providing them with healthier boundaries.

Never Be Afraid To Choose Your Path

One of the greatest lessons that I've learned, and I've watched my clients learn from their dogs, is about fully walking your own path. As I've used the Walk In Sync™ System, changing my clients over from their traditional training tools, it is so apparent that the issues that they're having with their dogs are also issues and challenges they're having in their lives—being hesitant to give directions or take charge, speaking up about what they require, and actually demanding what they want.

It has been astonishing to me to watch client after client transform behaviors. In the past, they were being less than the leaders that they truly are; they had developed habits of being too meek and forgiving on certain topics; and they were not being completely clear about what they wanted. Now each time I watch my clients step up to the plate, get a grip on their dogs using the Walk In Sync™ System, and really start to physically embody and exhibit their natural leadership within minutes, it's such a sight of beauty to behold. Previously those clients were physiologically in a place of feeling doubtful or questioning themselves or not feeling deserving of what they were asking for, not just from their dogs but in their lives.

All of this seems to change so quickly once they use Walk In Sync™. I've had clients come back to me to let me know how being able to take charge of their dogs helped them to actually take charge of their own lives.

A Friend in NYC

I have a very good friend who's a pet reporter in New York City, and also does pet rescue most favorably for pit bulls. After meeting one day on her city block, we put the Walk In Sync™ System on her little pit bull. This dog was very, very disconnected with himself. He had no real body awareness or true sense of confidence, but he was a strong dog and he would go out and try to lead the walk. Once we changed over to the Walk in Sync™ System, I started working with him and getting him reconnected with his body. As soon as this little pit bull realized the rules he needed to adhere to, I was confident that he could move through whatever he had been holding onto that was not allowing his greatest potential to come through. Well we worked for about ten minutes, taking a walk around the block. And he really started to make some very significant shifts.

When this little pit bull was ready, I handed him back to his mom. During the first couple of times that they started walking, her old habit resurfaced of checking in with him and wondering what he was going to do next. And each time something would come up, I would gently guide her back to the realization that she was in charge now and she should be leading the walk. I told her that once she sets the clear boundaries of where they're going on their walk and who's going to actually be in charge, then her dog will listen to her.

My friend wrote me a note a week later, saying, "This is so amazing because what I am finding is that not only has my dog changed significantly as he is paying way more attention to me, but I am stepping up to the plate and being a true leader to my dog, and it's helping me in every area of my life." It was one of the most rewarding emails I've ever received.

My friend had finally realized that use of the proper tools was all that was needed to make a smooth, almost imperceptible transition into becoming a leader to her dog. Being a facilitator who assists people as they transform into their dogs' leaders and then become leaders in their own lives is extremely gratifying to me. I'm sure you can see my smile right now.

"The dog has seldom been successful in pulling man up to its level of sagacity, but man has frequently dragged the dog down to his."
James Thurber

Secret # 6:

Harness Your Dog's Energy to Unleash His or Her Greatest Potential

Discipline Is Not a Four-Letter Word

I remember when I was a child and my parents would send me to my room for doing something bad. They would tell me, "Go to your room and think about what you did, and don't come out until you know." The truth is I sat there for a long time. I tried so hard to figure out what was wrong with me and what I had done that was bad. Surely I should have known, but I didn't.

It turns out I was a child in need of learning how to discipline and manage my energy so that I could unleash my greatest potential. I was not a child who needed to sit in my room and think about what I did that was wrong because I didn't know I was doing anything wrong, I was just being my full-of-energy seven-year-old self, just like I was supposed to be.

I remember being so frustrated bordering on angry with my parents because when you have a child or dog who is so full of energy that he needs to expend, one of the most detrimental things you can do is tell him to shut his energy off and make him sit and think rather than create or express himself through that energy.

What I needed as a child was guidance. I needed someone to understand that I was filled to the brim with the energy of creation, imagination, and exploration. I was young and needed to explore my world within safe, healthy boundaries. I needed someone to realize that what may have been more effective was to help me explore creative outlets for that energy that would allow me to discipline or channel it in constructive ways that would benefit me through my life.

This discipline of learning a new skill requires focus, total attention, presence in the moment, and willingness to become totally absorbed in what one is doing. This is how we discipline energy for the greatest benefit and mastery of a particular skill.

Maybe this frustrating situation prompted me to develop my Walk In Sync™ System as I could sense dogs' frustration at not understanding exactly what their people wanted from them. And being sensitive, I started to ask the dogs what worked best for them—what they needed from their people to clear up the communication disconnects I was observing taking place time and again.

I created the tools to allow for the greatest level of guidance and improved communication that translated into a type of discipline, but it's not a discipline that ever makes the dog wrong. It's a discipline that allows the dog specific boundaries to make the healthiest choices. When we talk about disciplining our dogs, it's not about yelling at them and it's not about making them wrong for certain behaviors. Instead, we're talking about a certain way to consistently apply a routine of behavior, allowing the dog to channel his/her energy in the healthiest of ways and excel within that place so that he/she can then take the foundation of that and move it into the next place when ready to develop more skills and excel. The entire point of healthy boundaries, discipline, and focus is to continually assist your dog in unleashing and achieving their greatest potential in a safe, effective, efficient manner.

As we learned as young children, discipline can have a bad connotation or it can be really beneficial to us. When I was in my early twenties and I started weight training, my ex-boyfriend taught me that true discipline is being dedicated to continuing a certain path every day and following a certain level of a routine. The reasoning was that if I were disciplined enough to weight train every day, then I would develop stronger muscles that would allow me to be a better athlete, enhance my conditioning, and improve my brain function and my life.

Anyone who knows anything about professional athletes knows that they are some of the most disciplined and focused people on the planet. They have to be in order to continue moving their energy in a certain direction that pushes the limits of their potential and allows them to be the greatest athletes possible. So the discipline that they apply is to a daily routine of channeling their energy in a certain way that allows them to excel at what they do. This is the same type of discipline that we want to apply to our dogs.

For example, when we say "no" it's a no; when we ask them for something, they've got three to five seconds to respond before they get a gentle correction. When we help our animals realize that discipline allows them more freedom, we will stay consistent in our actions with them. We will apply the discipline of approaching our dogs with a certain routine on a daily basis so it becomes a habit. And it becomes a gentle, fun habit that gives them more room because we discipline them enough to allow them to harness their energy in a certain beneficial way.

Learning to Harness Our Own Energy

When I was growing up, I had a very challenging time in school. I was extremely bored—school was not very stimulating and I really wasn't good at just taking information and spitting it back because most of the information really didn't make any sense to me in a practical application. As a result, I developed a lot of rebellion against the school system, against my parents for making me go to school, and against authority. None of this rebellion actually helped me learn how to harness and channel my own energy. It just set me up to continually rebel against anything that I did not understand.

When I started weight training in my early twenties, it was the first time in my life that I began to develop a type and a level of discipline that felt natural and conducive to my energy. This discipline allowed me to channel all of my energy, awareness, and intelligence in a constructive way where I could experience results that felt good and made sense to me. When I later began my training as a fitness instructor, I helped my clients do the same thing as I had. I helped them learn to stay focused, channel and harness their energy in a way that would actually support them and develop their maximum potential.

As I went in to my further into my Qi Gong Training, Dr. Lu helped me learn how to take all of this bounding creative energy and channel it into a form that would allow me greater success in helping people with their health, guiding them through the challenging spaces in their lives, while also helping them realize their greatest potential.

When I went into dog training, I started to realize that dogs are similar to a six- or seven-year-old child: bounding energy all over the place, wanting to see everything, be everywhere, and do everything. In order to have a dog who was trustworthy and on whom I could rely, in order to have a dog who I could feel safe enough to take off leash, I had to learn how to help my dog to harness his/her own energy. And in that process of learning how to help my dog harness this energy, I actually learned how to become more fully present and harness my own. I began to realize that I could have a million great ideas but I had to pick one or two to focus on. If I harnessed my energy and channeled it through those paths, something substantial could be created.

Working with dogs has given me such a unique opportunity to understand how best to harness my energy, keep myself thinking clearly, and utilize my greatest gifts. I have learned how to direct and guide my energy through the proper channels, which has allowed me to bring this information to you, to create Walk In Sync™, and to gain insights and awareness into how dogs really think and what actually motivates them.

Mindless Exercise vs. Mindful Exercise

All dogs and pups require exercise for a healthy body, clear mind, and balanced energy. This is a known fact. What I have discovered about exercise for dogs is that you can drain their energy through exercise or train and harness their energy through exercise of the right type.

When I am at the park it's easy to see balls and toys being thrown to happy pooches that love the repetition of bringing the objects back to their pleased humans. Some of the reasons they are so happy is that in their minds retrieving is a job (all dogs thrive having a job and clear direction), they are pleasing their people, and they are moving their bodies.

I am all for exercising every day but I have come to realize that when exercising your dog you want to exercise their minds as much as you do their bodies. When a dog is put on Walk In Sync™ what happens during the walk is that due to the boundaries of consistent leash length the dog's brain is constantly engaged to make choices to back off pressure as soon as they bump it. This engages the whole dog and harnesses the dog's energy in the most beneficial ways of mind-body exercise rather than just draining the dog's energy with body exercise of repetitive chasing.

There is definitely a difference between draining off excess energy through exercise and allowing the dog to harness and focus that energy through having to engage their mind on an entire walk. When a dog is taken out or to the park and the main method of draining the dog's energy is repetitive chasing, the dog will drain his/her energy, rest, and then the energy comes back even stronger. The increased stamina and intensity of the energy will require more repetition and if there is any misalignment in their structure it will cause increased wear and tear on their joints. It will also require more and more time to drain their energy. And if the weather changes and you can't get the dog out to the park for a few days you will have a dog with a lot of pent-up energy looking to channel it somewhere—hopefully not at your couch.

When I began working dogs on the Walk In Sync™ System what I noticed was that I only needed to walk a dog for maybe 15 to 30 minutes with consistent clear boundaries to exhaust them the first few walks. After their walks they slept like a rock, as if they had just been on a 1.5-hour hike uphill. But what I noticed afterward was even more astounding to me. The dogs I had worked were calmer with or without their daily walk. They had more patience, were more relaxed in their own bodies, and were more willing to take their cues from their humans' timeframe to get them out than their own inability to control their impulsive energy for exercise. And on days when the dogs could not get out as long due to inclement weather, they remained calm and were not bouncing off of the walls.

I found that when you exercise a dog's mind along with his body and teach him to harness that energy in an efficient, effective manner, then you have a dog who learns to channel that excess energy in the most beneficial ways that work for you both. Happy dog and happy human.

All Achievements Require Great Focus

Using discipline was the first step I had to learn to become fully aware of how to apply my energy each day, as it helped me continue to move through, expand, and grow my own being. One thing that was challenging to me in working with dogs was focusing. We all know that new puppies are actually similar to most adults today—they have about a four-second attention span. What I had to do was help them teach the puppies how to focus. But first I had to teach the people to learn to be present, to focus, and to be patient with the process. Essentially they needed to learn to harness their own energy in order to be great leaders to their dogs. Trust me, the puppies are way easier to work with!

Treat training was a great option—it gave pups a focus for a couple of seconds. It also taught me that focus is something that's built over time by disciplining your energy through practice. It's not something that's automatic. So when working with puppies, I began by only incorporating two- or three-minute sessions at the maximum. In these little mini-sessions I could introduce something to the puppy and allow him or her to learn it and then slowly build the puppy's focus day after day.

Focus is essential in training our dogs. Because it's so easy for them, with their superior senses of smell, sight, and hearing to get distracted, each day you should be incorporating another building block toward having your dog focus solely on you. One of the best ways that I have found to get dogs to focus is by helping them stay connected to their bodies. When I developed the harness system, I realized that many of the dogs were not really connected to their bodies. They were disconnected due to improper training or abuse or just poor foundational training. The traditional tools we use to train a dog are neck based. One quick yank is all that is needed to cause a physical disconnection in the dog's energy channels to the extent that the dog loses awareness of his/her body in space and time and suddenly has no idea of his/her size or strength.

I discovered that a front clip harness actually helped give the dogs a place of reconnection to come back into their bodies, thus vastly improving their awareness of their bodies in space and time and giving a much greater ability to focus without pain or discomfort. By setting a clear and unmovable boundary for the dog when pulling, the system provides a safe opportunity for the dog to become fully present and notice where his body is and make the choice to back off pressure at his choosing. Always remember that this is a huge tool to use in your dog training arsenal because with discipline and clarity of boundaries comes focus. Not only is it something that is beneficial for our dogs, but also it is also valuable for humans.

Client Story

I was called to work with a 160-pound Mastiff who had begun chasing people on bikes and was getting aggressive with smaller dogs. When speaking to his mom by phone, I knew it would be interesting because she talked a mile a minute and continued to tell me one thing and then made excuses for the dog when I got specific. I agreed to meet them at the dog park the following week.

The day arrived and I met the two at the park. To say this dog was enormous is an understatement (think mini-horse). I went inside the gate and he approached me in a bit of a Mastiff threatening way to see how I would react. As he came up I turned away, ignoring him and walking in a different direction. He was kind of curious with that response and just followed me while at the same time lowering his energy. His mom was about 10 feet away, yelling things at him, which he honestly could care less about.

As we chatted and I continued to assess the dog, while

hearing the litany of things "wrong" with the dog from his human, I asked her about how he grew up. Then came the confession. "I treated him like my baby. He was just such a cute puppy and I let him get away with everything because I couldn't get mad at him, I would just laugh. So maybe I am the one who created the problem and maybe you need to really work with me today more than him."

Side Note: I was really impressed she owned that. The dog was too big, too used to getting his way, and too much of an oversized baby. I would have to work with him and reset him first then bring her in on it and work with her. It is a lot easier to work with our dogs when they are young and want to please you then when they get older and have decided they want to please themselves. As I looked into this four-year-old dog's eyes I could see he was emotionally stuck at six months of age. He was confused about leadership and didn't want to be the leader, but what other choice did he have since his human was not stepping up to the plate.

As I said, this was a big boy, frightening and intimidating just by sheer size alone. Yet when I put the harness on him and started to walk with him away from his mom, he parked it and would not move. The baby, not the bully, was starting to reveal his true colors. It was amazing, the dog then proceeded to lie down and not move like a little six-month-old puppy. The thing he didn't realize was that I was not his mom, I had clear boundaries and I would be as patient as needed till he chose to let go of his resistance and move through his behavior.

The main thing that this dog did not receive from his attentive mom was a true awareness that he was not in charge, she was. He learned by her inability to be consistent and disciplined in working with him every day that he could get away with a lot. Now, though, a lot of that was turning into aggression and dangerous behaviors—not acceptable, on either account.

As I worked with him, he went through different episodes of lying down, trying to walk away from me, crying for his mom. What amazed me was that as he was doing all of these behaviors and I was staying disciplined with what I was asking him for, he was for the first time being given an opportunity to actually take responsibility for his misbehaviors and grow up and become the great dog that he is. By making him focus and teaching him to harness his energy in a disciplined manner, within 25 minutes of working him he had become a new dog. He had evolved from a latent six-month-old into the incredible four-year-old dog he is today. Using the harness helped me work him in a manner that was safe, reconnected him with his body, and allowed me to stay completely consistent the entire time we were working. The entire retraining process took less than 25 minutes.

Once I got him reset to the present moment, it was time to work with his mom. That is a whole other story. Let me just say, it is often far easier to work with dogs then it is humans. Humans like to stay vested in the rightness of their story. I had to work with his mom for 45 minutes to get her where she needed to be to be a great leader to this dog. The work was worth it—she really stepped up that day as did her dog. It was beautiful to finish the session watching the two of them Walk In Sync™ with the proper discipline that helped them both harness their energy to unleash their greatest potentials.

Practice Creates Greater Flow

When I started training my own dogs, I was told by the trainer that we would have to do an hour of training a day using repetitive conditioning and repeating the same commands. This trainer told me that having my dogs do the same commands over and over again is what would create great dogs. Well, I was bored and so were my dogs. What I began to do was break down the practice sessions and divide them into smaller increments, making them two to three minutes maximum. I wanted to keep it fun, keep it light, and show my dogs what I needed them to do. They did a great job and as soon as the training sessions were over, my dogs felt good and so did I. There was neither stress nor anxiety; it was really easy. So when working with your dogs, think about practicing maybe four or five times a day no longer than three or four minutes each time. And remember that practice makes perfect and creates a flow and an additional connection for you and your dogs to move through.

Trust Yourself

One thing that I have noticed over the years is that we humans don't always trust ourselves. We're continually asking for advice before doing the right thing and making the right decisions. When we lack trust in ourselves, our dogs also will lack trust in us. If we are not a clear, confident leader, our dogs are going to become their own leaders and going to rely on natural instincts. One of the major lessons that I have learned from my dogs is to trust myself. Once I listen to my intuition, my first gut feeling, and reaction, I'll develop a consistency of trust within myself. It's simple: If I trust myself, my dogs will trust me. If I don't trust myself, my dogs will not trust me. And my job is to set the foundation for dogs and people to trust each other.

Believe in Your Path

Every creature on this planet has a path specific to him or her. We don't always know exactly what that path is nor do we always know exactly what form it will take. The more that we trust our gut feelings, listen to our hearts, do what we love, and believe in ourselves, the more we are able to accomplish on our path. My dogs totally believe in what they're doing and where they're going. It is fascinating to me that they will actually give me their trust when they are on such a determined path to follow a scent. They've taught me that by believing in yourself and believing in your path, you can achieve anything you choose.

"Dogs are our link to paradise. They don't know evil or jealousy or discontent. To sit with a dog on a hillside on a glorious afternoon is to be back in Eden, where doing nothing was not boring--it was peace." - Milan Kundera

Opening to New Possibilities

Harnessing your dog's energy to unleash your dog's greatest potential with your own is a new possibility opening up in the training field for dogs.

In the dog training world there are many different theories about training methods. All have validity (some more than others) and some will work better for certain dogs than others. I am truly grateful to you for being open to receiving this information to use in your training toolbox.

It has been my personal experience that dogs don't understand science and theory, they understand energy. A silent energy is common to their entire species mind. This energy has several components: pictures, body language, use of energy, and vocalizations. Dogs know these rites and rituals far better than any human. Therefore any human theory or application we apply to dogs has its limitations.

What I have expressed in this book and through my Walk In Sync™ Method is what I have experienced as the most accurate interpretation of that energy I have observed during my 15 years of working with these amazingly insightful and loyal beings.

It is my hope that by learning about and embodying the 6 Secrets it will help you gain deeper insights into how to unleash your dog's greatest potential and, by practicing these secrets on a daily basis, unleashing your own.

Please feel free to pass those skills of Authentic Leadership onto your children, spouse, boss, friends, coworkers, colleagues, the rest of the world, and anyone else you choose to share this with.

Enjoy Walking In Sync™! **Paws up!**

Alecia

Appendix A

Two Veterinarians who are taking this issue seriously are Dr. Peter Dobias and Dr. Karen Becker, who have uncovered a study linking dog collars to seizures.

Dr. Peter Dobias, DVM

Why choke, prong, and shock collars can cause serious health issues

By Dr. Peter Dobias

Before you start reading the following lines, I invite you to do a little test. Open your hands with your thumbs touching each other. Place the thumbs at the base of your throat with the fingers pointing back and surrounding your neck. Now, take a deep breath, squeeze and pull back with all your force, keeping your thumbs connected.

This is how many dogs feel when they are on the leash and they are pulling.

If you are still keen to continue with this experiment, put a choke chain around your neck and attach it to a leash. Ask a friend to grab the end of the leash and pull and jerk on it periodically. Welcome to the dog world!

No, I will not make you go on with this experiment and ask you to test a prong collar or electric shock collar. I just want you to become more aware of what is happening. These types of dog collars have caused more injuries then you can imagine.

One day, Skai and I were on one of our favorite walks in Capilano Canyon near our home in North Vancouver. The wild river has carved the rock into breathtaking scenery with moss-covered cliffs, white water rapids, and old-growth rainforest.

Just a few minutes after starting our walk, I noticed a man with a young German shepherd on a leash. The poor little pup was struggling to say hi, however his human had a different idea. He was determined to prevent his dog from coming closer to us by yanking and jerking harshly on the leash that was attached to a choke chain. With every yank, I caught myself closing my eyes, cringing and feeling terribly sorry for the poor dog. He was coughing and gagging with every jerk and had no idea what was going on.

Suddenly the voice in my head whispered: "Peter, you must say something, this poor dog is helpless and will get hurt," the voice went on, "maybe the man is not even aware of what he is doing."

"Excuse me," I started with hesitation, "you may not be aware of this but the choke chain you are using can cause a lifelong injury and damage and I thought you may want to know why".

"Thank you, that would be great, I would love that," the man replied. "I had no idea."

Here is what our chat was about:

Wondering where the collar originated from?

No one really knows when the use of collars started. Perhaps it was the way the cave people restrained their wild dogs from running away. However, the first reference to dog collars comes from Ancient Egypt.

The reason why I am so weary of collars is that when dogs pull they can cause a lot of damage. The neck and cervical spine are one of the most important "energy channels" in the body. It contains the spinal cord for supply to the whole body, is where the front leg nerves originate from, and it is the energy channel where the nerves controlling the internal organ function pass through. The thyroid gland that regulates the whole body metabolism is also located in the neck.

For years, I have observed the relationships between the neck injuries and health of dogs. I have learned that if the flow of energy in the neck is interrupted or restricted, a whole array of problems may arise including lameness, skin issues, allergies, lung and heart problems, digestive issues, ear and eye conditions, thyroid gland dysfunctions to name a few. I also suspect that the patients that have severe energy flow congestion in the neck area have a higher cancer rates.

While the purpose of this article is not to give you long descriptions of each condition, I would like to give you a few examples to help you understand how important the health and alignment of the neck is to the general health of your dog.

Hypothyroidism (low thyroid gland hormone) may be related to collar related injuries.

For the longest time I have been puzzled about the high rates of thyroid issues in breeds that frequently pull on the leash, such as Labrador retrievers and German shepherds. It seems obvious that the collar actually pushes on the throat exactly in the area of the thyroid gland. This gland gets severely traumatized whenever a dog pulls on the leash, it becomes inflamed and consequently "destroyed" by the body's own immune system when it tries to remove the inflamed thyroid cells.

The destruction of the thyroid cells leads to the deficit of thyroid hormone—hypothyroidism and because the thyroid gland governs the metabolism of every cell. The symptoms may be low energy, weight gain, skin problems, hair loss, and a tendency to ear infections and organ failure.

Ear and eye issues are frequently related to pulling on the leash.

When dogs pull on the leash, the collar restricts the blood and lymphatic flow to and from the head. My clients are often perplexed when all the ear and eye problems disappear after switching their dog from a collar to the right harness.

Excessive paw licking and foreleg lameness can also be related to your dog's collar.

Leash pulling impinges the nerves supplying the front legs. This can lead to an abnormal sensation in the feet and dogs may start licking their feet. These dogs are often misdiagnosed as allergic and all that needs to be done is to remove the collar and treat the neck injury.

Neck injuries can cause a variety of problems.

Some dogs suffer severe whiplash like injuries from being jerked around. Extension leashes do not help because they encourage dogs to pull. They are faced with the imminent jerk when they get to the end of the line.

Most people do not know that leashes and collars can be at the core of many problems and that just one incident of pulling or running fast to the end of the leash can be serious. So how can we reduce such risk?

A harness--the collar alternative.

Over the years, I have searched for the best way of making dogs safe and to prevent neck injuries. Harnesses that have the leash attached at the front of the chest are the best solution because they distribute the pressure of tugs and jerks throughout the whole body and keep the neck and throat free.

Many harnesses on the market have the leash attached on the back and pulling still restricts the front portion of the neck thereby pressing on veins, arteries, nerves, and energy channels.

When you choose the right harness, make sure that your dog's harness is the right fit and follow the maker's instructions carefully. Use the harness only when leash walking and take it off when your dog is off leash. Ensure that the harness is not pressing or rubbing anywhere and that it is washed regularly.

http://peterdobias.com/community/2011/07/dog-collars-can-cause-disease-and-possibly-lead-to-cancer/

The Surprising Connection Between Pet Collars and Seizures by Dr. Karen Becker, DVM

Seizure Causes: There are a number of different causes of seizures.

Head trauma which results in brain swelling can cause seizures.

Brain tumors are a very common source of seizures in older pets. It's very unlikely your 12-year-old dog or cat will develop epilepsy. If you have a pet getting up in years who starts seizing, unfortunately, the likely cause is a brain tumor.

Bacterial, viral, fungal, and parasitic infections can also cause seizures.

Certain immune-mediated diseases can cause seizures.

Cervical subluxation can also cause seizures, and this is something many pet owners don't realize. I see this type of seizure a lot in dogs that are chained outside. They run out the length of their chain chasing after a bunny, and when the chain snaps back against the neck it causes a high cervical traumatic

injury of either the C1 vertebrae (the atlas) or C2 (the axis).

The C1 is the first cervical vertebrae in animals, and it articulates with the brain stem. When there is increased cerebrospinal fluid pressure in the brain stem, it can lead to a seizure.

I recommend you harness your pet not only for walks, but also if he's ever chained out. It's important your pet is not able to increase pressure on the neck, because high cervical subluxations and other chiropractic issues in the neck can caused an increased likelihood of seizures.

See Video:
http://healthypets.mercola.com/sites/healthypets/archive/20 11/02/22/pet-seizures-and-pet-dog-cat-food-diet.aspx

---

Q&A with Dr. Dodds: Can collars really damage the thyroid?

Dear Jean Dodds,

My name is Cindy and I live in the Netherlands. I just read something about dogs and pulling on the leash that it is very bad. I read it in Dutch and I read also your name on it.

Is it really so bad that a dogs pulls on a leash for his/hers thyroid? And here in the Netherlands they also said that it is bad for the eyes of a dog.

What kind of dog collar or harnass can I better use if my dogs pull on a leash?

Kind regards,

Cindy

Dr. Dodds Says:

Dear Cindy: Hello – this is an important question that we're all trying to pay more attention to, because the thyroid and salivary glands are superficially located just under the skin in the upper part of the neck. The thyroid gland is a butterfly-shaped organ just in front of the larynx and trachea, and the mandibular salivary glands are found on the side of the face just below the ears. Thus, they can be easily injured by trauma and sudden pressure forces (like could occur from the slip ring and chain of metal collar, and a metal prong or hard braided leather collar). A harness or "gentle leader" type collar is preferred these days, especially for strong dogs that like to pull and lunge out when on a standard collar and leash. Best wishes, W. Jean Dodds, DVM

W. Jean Dodds, DVM
Hemopet / NutriScan
11561 Salinaz Avenue
Garden Grove, CA 92843

View Article:
http://drjeandoddspethealthresource.tumblr.com/post/4164512158
5/dog-collars-thyroid

Other Products Available at www.WalkInSync.com

Walk In Sync™ System:

Humane Dog Walking and Training System that makes walking and training your dog a breeze without ever choking him or her.

Get A Grip Leash:

World's most comfortable leash. Accu-Grip™ handles allow for precision hand placement and provision of clear boundaries on every walk.

The In Sync™ Method: Home Study Course
6 Secrets Your Dog Wants To Teach You To Unleash Your Greatest Potential

For over 15 years, holistic dog trainer Alecia Evans has been successfully cultivating a unique inside perspective on training directly from the dogs themselves. In this home study course Alecia will share with you her breadth of work that has led to creating this intimate connection and teach you how to have it with your dog or pup.

"Baby You Were Born This Way" : Animal Communication Home Study Course

Over 18 years ago, Alecia began waking up to the gift of telepathic communication and her ability to directly communicate with the dogs. Alecia has gained an inside line to their awareness of how to most effectively train and bond with our dogs. In this home study course Alecia will teach you the simple yet powerful and profound tools to assist you in accessing your inner animal communicator.

Just Breathe Technique
www.TheJustBreatheTechnique.com

As an Elite fitness trainer and holistic health practitioner for over 18 years, Alecia realized that the #1 key to improving health, clarity, changing old patterns, connecting with nature, and being fully present is the breath. During the depth of her Qi Gong practice, Alecia was provided with the foundational tools that will assist anyone in rebalancing their health and tuning into their highest knowing and potential by learning how to breathe properly.

BioNutriton
http://www.bioage.com/cart.php?m=affiliate_go&affiliateID=
5a7855a997762bfbb6ae2f8af958c4c7&go=

One of the single best products I have ever used for a plethora of health issues. All dogs require enzymes in their food to assist with digestion, assimilation, and absorption. This product contains that and delivers high quality nutrition to assist your dog in maintaining optimal health.

UltraNano Health Solutions
www.ultrananohealthsolutions.com
Click on Pet Products by Alecia Evans

The products contained in this site are highly beneficial to assist in keeping your dog's mineral and electrolytes in a balanced state. The Molecula Silver is beneficial as an additional aid to any anti-biotic or any for any virus, fungus or parasites. I suggest the: Humic Acid complex, the Fulvic Acid complex and the Molecula Silver.

Testimonials

Alecia Evans' creation of the Walk-in-Sync™ harness technology is not just evolutionary, but revolutionary. It is way past due to have a safer harness technology that does not have the potential to injure a dog's neck and create musculoskeletal harm. That technology is now available thanks to the creative genius of Alecia Evans.

As a pioneer in Integrative Animal Health Care for 30 years, editor of the three veterinary textbooks "Complementary and Alternative Veterinary Medicine and Veterinary Acupuncture", two books on the human animal bond, I have always felt that there need to be more humane approaches to training as well as collars and harnesses. After reviewing Alecia's creation, I am most appreciative and realize that her invention is it.

I have many of my own ideas on innovative creations to help animals, but I have never seen anything like the Walk-In-Sync™.
-Dr. Allen Schoen, DVM

We highly recommend the Walk in Sync™ Humane Dog Walking and Training System.
-Gail Fisher, Owner All Dogs Gym

It transforms the act of walking my dog into walking with my dog.
-Paris Permenter, Publisher of DogTipper.com

What makes this system different from other front harnesses is that it allows full movement of front legs and it helps redirect your dog's attention back in the direction of the human at the other end of the leash.
-Dr. Sophia Yin, Dr. Yin's Animal Behavior and Medicine http://goo.gl/F6Ydm

I am having so much success with the Walk in Sync™ System that I need to order more!
-S. Hopmans, Therapeutic Pets of Santa Barbara

We use the Walk in Sync™ System on Dister and he is a perfect gentleman. For a dog who is never on a leash that is a miracle.
-R. Rose, Basalt, Colorado

I tried other flexible "training" harnesses that pulled tight under her legs and rubbed her raw, rear-attaching "walking" harnesses that gave me better leverage to pull her back but never stopped her from pulling. I've tried leash techniques that were uncomfortable for both me and Heidi. Nothing took. But literally the first walk we took in the Walk in Sync™ System Heidi stopped **herself** from pulling. Thank you so much, from the bottom of my heart, for giving me the dog I always knew was in her.
-Audra Alexander

OMG! Thank you Thank you Thank you! We walked approximately 2 miles, and might I add 2 glorious miles with absolutely NO PULLING! It was such a peaceful, enjoyable walk...from start to finish!. With this harness and lead she literally started out at my left leg and remained there streets....I was thrilled and I think once we returned home she was even much happier and relaxed then on previous walks. It was almost as if somehow she had had a burden lifted from her, that she no longer needed to be 'the front man' for our outings.

So thank you doesn't seem adequate...I hope just the thought that yet another human/dog duo are able to venture out into the great outdoors and truly enjoy their walks communing with nature! With much gratitude...Happy Tails To You!
-Kendra & Ziva

Thank you Alecia for this great invention! I'm the owner of two crazy, hyper, wild boxers.... I've never enjoyed walking them due to embarrassment, being scared they would get out of harness or drag me down the street. We tried them all and none worked...Thank you so very much! I love these harnesses. Raleigh and Annie can finally be walked again!
-Tracie and Jerry, Colorado

I used to run, frantically panting, behind my dog. Now we walk calmly together, side by side.
-Julia Szabo, The Pet Reporter, Author of *The Underdog – A Celebration of Mutts, Animal House Style, Pretty Pet Friendly* and Dogster.com Columnist

Your Walk-In-Sync™ Harness worked like magic!
-Andi Brown, Author of *The Whole Pet Diet: Eight Weeks to Great Health for Dogs and Cats* and Founder of Halo, Purely for Pets.

ABOUT THE AUTHOR

Alecia Evans is America's *Animal Heeler*. If Dr. Doolittle, Dr. Phil and Dear Abbey had a love child, it would be Alecia. Part Holistic Dog Trainer, Professional Animal Wellness Consultant, and Relationship Coach for humans and their animal companions, she consults with clients the world over, offering natural, safe, effective, holistic options and education on the topics of: health, emotional, and behavioral issues concerning their animals.

Her philosophy is: **harness your dog's energy to unleash their greatest potential and your own in the most natural manner possible.** Using her **Authentic Leadership** approach she has successfully transformed the relationship of hundreds of dogs of all ages, breeds and temperaments with their people, using her 6 Secrets approach that the dogs taught her to share with their people to help them unleash their dog's greatest potential and their own.

Alecia is evolutionizing the dog training world with her exclusive **In Sync™ Training Method.** As the leading expert in Humane Training Tools, she teaches people how to be in sync with their dogs in just minutes . Alecia is the author of: **The In Sync™ Method: 6 Secrets Your Dog Wants To Teach You To Unleash Your Greatest Potential.** Never feeling right about choking dogs and unsuspecting puppies to train them, Alecia invented **The Walk In Sync™ Humane Dog Walking and Training System** as the gold standard of training tools in order to end the choking of dogs during training and walking.

As an Animal Wellness Consultant over the last 15 years, Alecia has assisted hundreds of animals in regaining their physical and emotional health and vibrancy utilizing nature's pharmacy of supplements and natural remedies to address the animal's root issue and restore balance to their system and behavior.

She is an award winning TV and Radio Host, featured columnist, author, lecturer and workshop presenter on Natural Dog Training. Her work has been featured on: Fox and Friends, The Sandra Glosser Show, Plum TV and in Aspen Magazine, Dogtipper.com, The New York Daily News and Woof Report. She is the training expert for Dogtipper.com, The Big Bark, and a columnist for Pup Culture Magazine.

Alecia is the founder of National Train Humane Day, a world-wide virtual campaign to evolving the tools we use to train and walk dogs and pups to be humane and pain free. Alecia believes prevention and proper education about the best training methods and tools will begin to limit the number of dogs given up for adoption.

She currently resides in the Rocky Mountains of Colorado with her dogs and 2 horses. She can be reached at: info@dogwalkinsync.com

www.WalkInSync.com

Front and Back Cover Design: Marcello Alvarado

Cover Photo: Susan Drinker, www.drinkerdurrance.com

Bio Photo: Molly M. Peterson, www.mJmphotography.biz

Book Layout: Molly M. Peterson, www.mollympeterson.com

Made in the USA
Lexington, KY
05 February 2015